Inclusive Classrooms from A to Z:

A Handbook for Educators

Gretchen Goodman

TEACHERS' PUBLISHING GROUP
COLUMBUS • OHIO

Printed in the United States of America
99   6 5

Distributed by Crystal Springs Books
Box 500, Ten Sharon Road
Peterborough, NH 03458
800-321-0401

The pages of this book are printed on recycled paper containing a minimum of 10% post-consumer waste.

Publisher Cataloging-in-Publication Data

Goodman, Gretchen.
    Inclusive Classrooms from A to Z: A Handbook for Educators / Gretchen Goodman – 1st ed. -- Columbus, OH: Teachers' Publishing Group, 1994.
    [214]p : ill. ; cm.
    Includes bibliography.
    Summary : Goodman aims to give practical guidance to teachers as they strive to achieve a vision of schools as places where all children can experience success, develop lifelong friendships, and gain skills to enable them to become contributing members of society.
    ISBN 1-57110-200-0
    1. Teaching. 2. Learning. I. Title
    371.302' 82--dc20   1994   CIP

Library of Congress number is available from the publisher by request.

The following have generously given permission to use material in this book: adapted portions of handouts and graduate course requirements (Needs Assessment at the Classroom Level, Parent Program Preference Inventory, and Adaptations for Students with Disabilities) from Pennsylvania's Gateways Technical Assistance Initiative. "Circle of Friends" and "MAPS" adapted from *Educating All Students in the Mainstream of Regular Education*, edited by Susan Stainback, William Stainback, and Marsha Forest with permission of Evelyn Lusthaus, Marsha Forest, Jack Pierpont, and Paul Brookes Publishing Company. "The Cost of Inclusion" by Pat Jones from *Parent to Parent Newsletter*, reprinted with permission of Missouri Parents Act (MPACT).

Photos by Harry Goodman. Illustrations by Ed Francis, Jennifer Cary, and Jonathan Eshenour.
    Reproduction of activities, checklists, and forms for classroom use is permissible. Reproduction of any material in this book for commercial use, for an entire school or school system, or for any other purpose is strictly prohibited.

Dedication

This book is dedicated with love and appreciation to my husband Harry for his patience and understanding while I pursued this mission.

Acknowledgements

A special thank you to Dr. Barbara Hasson, the first person to take a chance on me in my new life; to my daughter Aimee, who is the greatest gift I have ever received; to Carlton Hoke, my Mac man; to Jean Mann for her constant encouragement; to my supportive principal, Rita Lane, who is a true champion for all children; to my parents who always believed I could do anything; to Debbie Sumner for her editing expertise; to members of The Society For Developmental Education family for the many doors they've opened; and most especially to Jim Grant, my mentor, who truly believes in teachers and their ability to provide children with successful school experiences.

In Memory of

In Memory of John Skillan, my dearest friend, who taught me the true definition of friendship, the meaning of acceptance and belonging, and more importantly, to hold on to the dream even when faced with life's most difficult challenges.

Table of Contents

Introduction .... *xi*

A: Acceptance *1*
   Tips 2
   Activity – *Naomi Knows It's Springtime* 4
   Activities for Promoting Acceptance 5
   Acceptance/Awareness Balloons 5
   How's Your Attitude Toward Accommodating Differently-Abled
      Students? (blackline master) 7

B: Belonging *13*
   Tips 14
   Activity – *It's George* 15
   Activities to Enhance Feelings of Belonging 16
   Letter from Denise (included child's perspective) 17

C: Cooperation *19*
   Cooperative Groups Activity 20
   33 Ways to Applaud Your Teammates (blackline master) 21
   33 Ways to Encourage Your Teammates (blackline master) 22

D: Diversity *23*
   Tips 24
   Activity Ideas 25
   Activity – *People* 26
   Activity – Color Hunt (blackline master) 27
   Diversities That May Be Present in the Regular Education Setting 28
   Children in the Classroom Are More Alike Than Different
      (Venn Diagram) 30

E: Evolution of Excellence *31*
   Tips 32
   Sample Schedules – Years One and Two 33
      Years Three and Four 34
      Year Five 35
      Primary Grades Support Schedule 36
      Intermediate Grades Support Schedule 37
   Fitting the Pieces Together 38
   The Inclusion Change Process 39

F: Friendship *41*
   Tips 42
   Circle of Friends Activity (blackline master) 43
   Student Interest Survey (blackline master) 45
   Classroom Directory (blackline master) 46

G: Gifts of All *47*
   Classroom Milestones Book 48
   Classroom Yellow Pages Directory (blackline master) 49

H: Helping Each Other *51*
    Tips 52
    Wheelchair Safety 54
        Wheelchair Safety Certificate (blackline master) 55
    Peer Tutoring Program 56
        Invitation Letter 57
        Letter to Volunteer Tutors (blackline master) 58

I: Individualized Education Program/Plan (IEP) *59*
    Best Practices in IEP Development (blackline master)................61
    IEP Inventory/Parent Questionnaire (blackline master) 62

J: Jargon *65*

K: Kicking Off the Project *67*
    Tips 68
    Developing an Action Plan 69
    16 Skills a Staff Needs for Successful Inclusion 70
    Inclusion Education Journey: A School-based
        Continuum to Assist in Planning for a Successful
        Inclusive Program (blackline master) 71

L: Lesson Adaptations *75*
    Tips 76
    Sample Accommodations...77
    In-Class Adaptations...78
    Aimee's Day 79

M: Maps *81*
    The MAPS Process 83
    MAPS Meeting Plan (blackline master) 84

N: Neighborhoods *85*
    Tips 86
    Letter from Kelsey (sibling perspective) 87

O: Organizing *89*
    Tips 90
    Chair Packs and Pockets...92
    Student Needs Assessment (blackline master) 93
    Inclusive Needs Assessment (blackline master) 94

P: Parents *101*
    Tips 102
    Sample Parent Letter 103
    Letter from Pat Jones (parent perspective) 104
    A Preamble to the IEP 105
    Elementary Inventory of Parent Preferences..............................106

Q: Questions *113*
    Ten Most Commonly Asked Questions Regarding
        Inclusion 113
    Inclusive Education Checklist 119

R: Rules *123*
    Tips 124
    Developing Rules with Your Class 125
    Sample Rules 126

S: Support *127*
    Tips 129
    Using Support Personnel in Your Room............................... 130
    Checklist to Monitor Included Children's Progress
        (blackline master) 131
    Student Profile Sheet (blackline master) 132
    A Principal's Observation Guide for the Inclusive,
        Natural Language Classroom (blackline master) 133

T: Teams *137*
    Tips 139
    Team Meeting Outline 140
    Scheduling Time for Team Meetings..................................... 141
    Instructional Support Team Meeting – Notice to
        Parents (blackline master) 142
    Developing Meeting Agenda and Goals (blackline master) 143
    Instructional Support Team Action Plan (blackline master)....144
    Support Planning (blackline master) 145

U: Utilizing Resources *147*
    Tips 148
    Staff Inventory – Sharing Your Expertise (blackline master)...149

V: Visitations *151*
    On-site Visitation Questionnaire (blackline master) 152

W: Why Inclusion *155*
    Inclusive Rationale 156
    Letter from Jonathan (included child's perspective)................ 157

X: Expectations *159*
    Common Developmental Expectations 160

Y: Your Strengths *163*

Z: Zero Rejection *165*
    Tips 166
    Levels of Student Participation 167
    Determining a Child's Level of Participation........................... 168

Appendix *169*
    Sample Evaluation Report 170
    IEP Inventory 173
    MAPS Meeting Plan 176
    Elementary Inventory of Parent Preferences 177
    Student Profile Sheet 184
    Sample IEP – Life Skills and Learning Support 185
    Support Planning.. 191
    Instructional Schedule 192

Professional Bibliography 193
Children's Bibliography 195
Organizations/Resources 197
About the Author...199

Introduction

Inclusion: the act of including or belonging, being together from beginning to end (American Heritage Dictionary, 1982).

Inclusion is the foundation of the life we lead, the preamble to quality life, and the removal of passports to segregation. From the moment of birth until the time of death, each living being has the intrinsic need to be included in society.

However, through societal oversight we have excluded differently-abled students in our school setting from becoming part of a true school community. Repeatedly, children with special needs have been sequestered in private schools, in isolated classrooms or in traditional pull-out programs. The foundation for such thinking has been rooted in our fear of the unknown. As "regular" classroom teachers, we have been instilled with the perception that we are not "special teachers" and therefore cannot teach those with special needs.

Inclusion education will eliminate segregation of the differently-abled and change our perceptions about what they and we can do. All across the nation, teachers are now embracing the idea of inclusion.

Inclusion is:

1. the belief that all children, gifted, at risk, physically, emotionally, and profoundly handicapped be included for all or part of the day in a regular classroom setting and have needs met in this classroom

"Inclusion education will eliminate segregation of the differently-abled and change our perceptions about what they and we can do."

2. treating all children equally in the classroom

3. designing a classroom to accentuate the success of all its members

4. the source for future relationships and for lifelong friendships

Many differently-abled children will grow up to work side by side with classmates who need to develop an attitude of acceptance.

That realization dawned on me in 1990 as I watched a young man who was unable to speak struggle with his wheelchair in the busy intersection of Pioneer Square in Seattle, Washington. All of us who were standing at the bus stop watching traffic move his way began to turn our heads. The reason (?) fear and uncertainty. We were unsure how to help this man, how to communicate with him, or how to properly steer a wheelchair. Our paths had never crossed with those who were differently-abled. In our school experience, differently-abled children had been placed in a special setting; our interactions with such individuals had been limited and our social uncertainties were increased.

As I boldly ran out to help this young man and not so gently got him over the curb, I was convinced that we are doing a disservice to our young children if we do not foster acceptance of diversity and eliminate fear of the unknown especially when dealing with peers who may present themselves differently.

This incident forced me to evaluate what was happening in schools today. I realized that in twenty years of teaching, I had never been asked to deal with a differently-abled child. If someone appeared in my kindergarten, first grade, or second grade class and didn't quite fit the mold academically, socially, physically, or developmentally, I set the wheels in motion to find a different placement for that child, perhaps in a special class down the hall or in a different school. I was guilty of excluding students because of a label and resistant to the new buzzword "inclusion" because I thought it would be more work for me. I didn't have time to learn new teaching techniques, and I certainly wasn't excited about having to team teach or collaborate with specialists.

But after returning home from Washington, I knew that I wanted to find out more about inclusion. I began attending conferences and taking college courses. I became involved in a state-wide program of providing instructional support to differently-abled children in the regular classroom and assisting teachers with instructional adaptations to ensure success for all children in the regular education setting. I have since worked in other schools in my district, in my home state of Pennsylvania, and throughout the country.

This has been a difficult journey for all of us involved in my school. Classroom teachers exhibited fears about not being competent to deal with differently-abled children. They were already feeling burned out with the constant changes in education. We had been implementing a whole language philosophy for five years, developmentally appropriate practices for three years and had revised our report cards two years earlier. Now this! Special needs children had been served by teachers who were trained in this area. Not only were we going to bring differently-abled children back to their home schools and classrooms, we were now going to begin a program of services that were "push ins" and not the comfortable "pull outs."

The successes, failures, and frustrations that we dealt with made me realize that many teachers are often asked to do the semi-impossible. We will do it, we can do it, but we often need help and support to guide us through any major paradigm shift.

That is the purpose of this book – to share practical guidance to teachers as they strive to achieve a vision of inclusive schools as places where all children can experience success, develop lifelong friendships, and gain skills that enable them to become contributing members of society.

This book provides background information on inclusion to reduce your fears, many hands-on activities and strategies for immediate implementation, and blackline masters, forms and checklists to help get you started. I've also answered the ten questions teachers from all over the country have most frequently asked about inclusion.

As you begin your journey of discovery, keep in mind that inclusion is a process of gradual change, not an event that will occur overnight. Inclusion is an important step toward a quality education and a quality life for all. It will ensure that our children do not look the other way when a friend needs help.

"Inclusion is an important step toward a quality education and a quality life for all."

A: ACCEPTANCE

Accepting children with diverse learning needs in the classroom today will help them feel secure in learning situations or social settings tomorrow.

The first step for those beginning inclusion is allowing time for teachers to share ideas, plan projects together, and develop goals to enhance the acceptance of all children in the classroom.

Accepting diversity as an asset is an essential part of making the plan work. Labels will disappear for both students and teachers and will no longer be the curriculum's driving force. All educators will become special educators and meet the individual needs of a wide range of learners.

If children are to learn how to accept others with diverse learning styles and needs, teachers must act as role models and teach by what they do – not merely by what they say. The positive manner of greeting children in the morning will set the tone for learning. By focusing on individual talents and gifts of each child entering the classroom, teachers will encourage students to work to the best of their abilities.

"Accepting diversity as an asset is an essential part of making the plan work."

Acceptance Tips

1. Hold before-school gatherings for coffee and informal sharing among staff and administrators.

2. Maintain a diverse selection of trade books that address acceptance and differences. Sharing children's literature such as *The Ugly Duckling* by Hans Christian Anderson, *Dinah, The Dog With A Difference* by Esta de Fossard, and *Naomi Knows It's Springtime* by Virginia Kroll (see activity on page 4) can help heighten student acceptance of differences. (See children's bibliography for other titles.)

3. Check with support personnel to make sure they feel accepted and comfortable in the classroom.

4. Encourage children to express their feelings and reactions in journal writing.

5. Allow children to change reading buddies every few days.

6. Develop individual goals for students to increase self-esteem or self-motivation. (This week Carrie will find two new friends to book share with, or John's goal is to teach two friends how to snap.)

7. Develop an "I Can" bulletin board. Place individual pictures of class members on the board. Place a push pin under each picture. Invite children to choose a sample of their schoolwork each Friday that exemplifies what they can do.

8. Design classroom T-shirts. Students may collectively choose a class logo, "Miss Stopper's class cannot be stopped from learning," or "Learning with Miss Monos is a 1, 2 bonus." Children can use iron-on crayon pictures or puff paint for designing. T-shirts are worn first day of each month.

9. Encourage adults to speak about a student's placement as a grade or class, not a place. Aimee is in the primary school, not Aimee is in an autistic group.

10. Describe a child as a child first, not as a disability. "Ryan is an eight-year-old with severe disabilities," not "Ryan is a severely-disabled child."

11. Invite adult community members with disabilities to talk to the class. We had an adult with cerebral palsy read a story to our class. He then demonstrated how he needed to hold a piece of chalk to outline the story and how to use a facilitated communication device.

12. When possible assign all children the same chores throughout the school year.

13. Set up classroom furniture to accommodate special needs children within the hub of learning rather than in the back of the room.

14. Vary expectations for journal writing and reading according to children's needs and abilities. For example, while some children write lengthy journal entries, others can cut and paste pictures to show feelings. While groups of children read and share literature, others can look at pictures, listen to stories on tape, or match pictures to words.

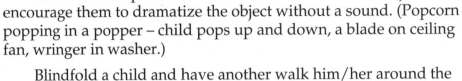

Acceptance Activity

Naomi Knows It's Springtime by Virginia Kroll

Purpose:

To enable children to accept different ways to interact with the environment and heighten their awareness of children with visual impairment.

Procedure:

Introduce children to *Naomi Knows It's Springtime* (Boyds Mills Press, 1993) by reading the story and allowing children to then hear it on tape.

Play "I Hear" game. Tape a variety of household sounds and have children attempt to identify sounds without knowing what is producing them.

Give students picture cards of common household objects and encourage them to dramatize the object without a sound. (Popcorn popping in a popper – child pops up and down, a blade on ceiling fan, wringer in washer.)

Blindfold a child and have another walk him/her around the room and describe common objects for guessing. "It's silver, it hangs on the wall, you turn it, you put a pencil in it to be sharpened."

Describe some ways Mrs. Jensen would have responded differently if Naomi had been deaf.

Allow children to buddy up and go for "trust walks" around the school with one child leading a blindfolded partner.

Use names of classmates for a "knows" book. Jennifer knows her ABC's. Jennifer knows her phone number and address.

Borrow an ice cream freezer and make frozen chocolate custard that Naomi liked.

Cut apart "Naomi knows" sentences and match to pictures.

Activities for Promoting Acceptance

1. Arrange students in a circle. Invite two children to stand in the center. Discuss similarities and differences.

2. Have two children pair up. They look at each other and take turns discussing what they like. Then the two children turn back-to-back, change something about their physical appearance, and see if the other person can identify the change.

3. Give children a challenging task (art project, sewing card). Set up the task so each child needs to ask two others for help. The two helpers sign the project to ensure that all classmates feel accepted enough to ask for help.

Acceptance/Awareness Balloons

Hang a balloon cutout each week on the door of your classroom to dispel myths about differently-abled people. Take time to discuss the sentiments expressed. Hang the balloons on a large bulletin board, accumulate throughout the year.

Sample statements for balloons:

1. Everyone in here is as important as everyone else.

2. Each classroom member has something positive to contribute to our group.

3. Physical challenges are not contagious. (You can't "catch" one like you can't "catch" hair color.)

4. Everyone can and will make mistakes sometimes.

5. We are more alike than we are different.

6. What's inside us (feelings, emotions, ideas) are more important than what's outside us (hair color, eye color, size of our house).

7. We all have some kind of weakness and must learn how to overcome it.

8. Some differences are short-term (glasses, braces, dark baby teeth, a broken wrist) and some may be forever (deafness, blindness, muscle paralysis).

9. Mental and physical challenges don't erase feelings.

10. You can see some reminders of people's limitations (wheelchairs, hearing aids, white canes). Other limitations are invisible (memory problems, dyslexia, autism).

11. We can work together to help our friends be successful.

12. None of us is as smart as all of us.

13. Each day is a new beginning for our class.

14. Try not to guess what a person is like on the inside by looking at the outside. (Don't judge a book by its cover.)

15. Do your feelings or abilities change if you get a bump on your knee?

16. What if everyone with brown hair had to go to a separate classroom or eat alone?

17. Knowing we are alike and different will help us be successful adults.

18. If you couldn't see, would you still want to have the same friends?

19. Being different is not an excuse for lack of work.

20. What if we all did only what we are good in?

21. I wish I could change _____ about myself.

22. We sink or swim together as a team.

23. Two heads are better than one.

24. Do you have the same needs or desires when you are clean as when you are dirty?

25. If someone looks or acts differently because of an impairment, it is not a punishment for being bad.

26. We can talk about differences with our friends if we do it respectfully.

27. Having a handicap or disability is only a tiny part of a person's being – just like a piece of sand is a tiny part of a beach.

28. It is more polite to talk about differences kindly than it is to point, stare, or giggle.

29. Many children with different needs have to work twice as hard as you do to get their work done.

30. Who in this room is exactly like you?

31. Name three ways you are different now than when you were one-year-old.

32. More things in here are possible than impossible.

33. We all learn in different ways.

34. Changing a little might save a lot of work.

35. We all make progress every day.

 Teachers' Publishing Group

How's Your Attitude Toward Accommodating Differently-Abled Students?

	I have arrived!	I am working on this	I do not believe this is possible	I am not prepared to deal with this
1. I respect students with disabilities as individuals with differences as I respect all children in my classroom.	☐	☐	☐	☐
2. I am aware of the individual capabilities of students and adapt accordingly.	☐	☐	☐	☐
3. I establish routines appropriate for students with disabilities (establish settings so children know what is consistently expected).	☐	☐	☐	☐
4. I employ classroom management strategies that are effective with students with disabilities (e.g., time out, point systems, etc.).	☐	☐	☐	☐
5. I consciously provide reinforcement and encouragement (e.g., encourage effort, provide support if student gets discouraged, emphasizing positive gains).	☐	☐	☐	☐
6. I attempt to determine student interests and strengths and connect personally with students.	☐	☐	☐	☐
7. I help students of all abilities learn to find appropriate avenues to express feelings and needs (drawings, sign language, time outs, etc.).	☐	☐	☐	☐
8. I am comfortable communicating with students with disabilities (plan frequent, short, one-on-one conferences, discuss potential modifications).	☐	☐	☐	☐

How's Your Attitude Toward Accommodating Differently-Abled Students?

	I have arrived!	I am working on this	I do not believe this is possible	I am not prepared to deal with this
9. I am comfortable communicating with the special education teacher (e.g., write notes back and forth, talk informally, collaborate during allotted prep time).	☐	☐	☐	☐
10. I communicate with parents of students with or without disabilities (e.g., write notes back and forth, talk informally, encourage them to provide support for student's education).	☐	☐	☐	☐
11. I expect the best from all students in the classroom and am aware of their capabilities.	☐	☐	☐	☐
12. I am able to make adaptations for students when developing long-range (yearly/unit) plans (e.g., establish realistic long-term objectives).	☐	☐	☐	☐
13. I consciously make adaptations for students when planning daily activities, being aware of potential problems before they occur.	☐	☐	☐	☐
14. I plan assignments and activities that allow students with and without disabilities to be successful (structure assignments to reduce frustration).	☐	☐	☐	☐
15. I strive to allot time for teaching successful strategies as well as content material (test-taking skills, note-taking skills).	☐	☐	☐	☐
16. I adjust the physical arrangements of room for students with disabilities (modify seating arrangements, provide space for movement).	☐	☐	☐	☐

How's Your Attitude Toward Accommodating Differently-Abled Students?

	I have arrived!	I am working on this	I do not believe this is possible	I am not prepared to deal with this
17. I construct study guides, tape-record readings, provide skeletal outlines, and hands-on activities for classroom members.	☐	☐	☐	☐
18. I am able to use alternative materials for learners (variety of textbooks, supplemental readers, calculators).	☐	☐	☐	☐
19. I encourage students to use computers for word processing or skill development.	☐	☐	☐	☐
20. I allow time to monitor the students' understanding of directions and assigned tasks (ask children to repeat or demonstrate what I have asked them to do, check in with students to be sure they are performing assignments correctly).	☐	☐	☐	☐
21. I observe students' understanding of concepts presented in class (attend to, comment on and reinforce understanding of vocabulary, abstract ideas, key words, time sequences, and content organization).	☐	☐	☐	☐
22. I provide individual instruction for students as needed (plan for one-on-one sessons after school, allocate time for individual instruction during class, provide cross-age tutoring).	☐	☐	☐	☐
23. I pair students of all abilities with peers to assist with assignments, projects, provide role models for behavior, academics and social interaction.	☐	☐	☐	☐

How's Your Attitude Toward Accommodating Differently-Abled Students?

	I have arrived!	I am working on this	I do not believe this is possible	I am not prepared to deal with this
24. I involve students in active learning and in cooperative learning groups of mixed abilities.	☐	☐	☐	☐
25. I encourage students of all abilities to participate in whole-group instructions.	☐	☐	☐	☐
26. I consciously provide extra time for students to process information and complete tasks.	☐	☐	☐	☐
27. I am comfortable breaking down assignments into smaller chunks to lessen frustration and ensure success.	☐	☐	☐	☐
28. I observe students in groups and individually, documenting progress and interaction.	☐	☐	☐	☐
29. I collect a variety of work samples from students which reflect progress and growth.	☐	☐	☐	☐
30. I conference with students to provide one-to-one feedback regarding individual achievement.	☐	☐	☐	☐
31. I adapt assessment prodedures as needed to ensure success (oral test, open book test, shortened test, more time for completion).	☐	☐	☐	☐
32. I am comfortable employing individual criteria for student assessment.	☐	☐	☐	☐
33. I present material to a variety of learning modalities within the classroom (auditory, visual, kinesthetic, tactual).	☐	☐	☐	☐

How's Your Attitude Toward Accommodating Differently-Abled Students?

	I have arrived!	I am working on this	I do not believe this is possible	I am not prepared to deal with this
34. I am comfortable collaborating with support personnel.	☐	☐	☐	☐
35. I am comfortable with support services provided in my classroom.	☐	☐	☐	☐
36. I am able to share gifts, talents and needs of my students with colleagues.	☐	☐	☐	☐
37. I see the job description of "teacher" as one who facilitates learning for children of all learning ability levels.	☐	☐	☐	☐
38. I embrace the philosophy that each child is important and worthwhile, demonstrating fulfillment of individual responsibilities while supporting one another.	☐	☐	☐	☐
39. I believe that all children belong and are capable of learning in the mainstream of school and community.	☐	☐	☐	☐
40. I value all children and their contributions to society.	☐	☐	☐	☐

B: BELONGING

Once teachers and classmates have accepted the value of diversity, the next challenge facing a teacher in an inclusion project is how to make all children feel that they belong. To a young child, feeling part of a group is much more important than memorizing the two times tables or knowing the short vowel sounds. Helping children develop a sense of belonging while making lifelong friendships is an educational priority of inclusive schools.

According to noted counselor and psychologist Linda Albert (1989), students need to feel capable of successfully reaching school goals, to connect with peers and adults, and to contribute to the success of the group as a whole.

Teachers report that eliminating the "us" vs. "them" barriers from competitive classrooms and building a community spirit enhances children's feelings of belonging.

Children who feel they belong in a classroom build on each other's success, take pride in their class, enjoy being helpers, and behave appropriately.

"Helping children develop a sense of belonging while making lifelong friendships is an educational priority of inclusive schools."

Belonging Tips:

1. Involve all students, parents, and staff in school life.
2. Refer to all students and teachers by name, not label.
3. Interact with all students in the school, not just your own class.
4. Have a school suggestion box to express concerns and share solutions.
5. Display everyone's work.
6. Hold a regular classroom forum to evaluate the progress your class is making as a team.
7. Assure the child that s/he will move on to the next grade with peers.
8. Plan on children arriving and leaving at the same time.
9. Encourage included children to participate in after-school activities such as Brownies, Cub Scouts, latch key, etc.
10. Encourage children to be cross-age tutors, wheelchair drivers, and classroom helpers. Ask them to share their experiences with other classes.
11. Guidance counselors can develop a Friendship Club or a New Neighbor's Club to promote small group skills for belonging and making friends.

Belonging Activity

It's George by Miriam Cohen

Have each child's hand traced and cut out. Write the child's name in the center of the hand. Pass the hands around the classroom to five different friends. Each friend writes a positive comment on a finger. The completed hand is returned to the owner.

Encourage the class to brainstorm different ways George could have been included during class project time. List suggestions on chart paper.

Assign the class a special team project. Cut designated shapes in half. Children match halves and meet their partner. Projects are completed in pairs while all feel a sense of belonging.

Discuss as a class how George would have reacted differently had Mr. Emmons fallen down the steps.

Invite an ambulance crew to talk to the class regarding 911 services.

Review addresses and phone numbers of all children in the class.

Have a simulated newscast in the classroom. Children could

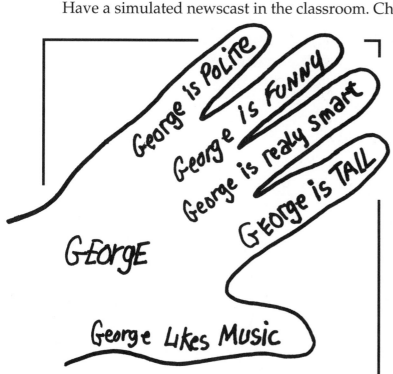

role play being an announcer and interviewing their partner with questions such as, "Tell me two ways you helped _____ feel like he (or she) belonged in your class." "Tell me how this class helps new students feel welcomed."

Other Activities to Enhance Feelings of Belonging

1. Model and role play situations regarding put downs, negative, and positive classroom scenarios.

2. Children design personal name tag or buttons for tables, coat hooks, mailboxes.

3. Videotape all children in a variety of class projects. Send the tape home to a different family each night so children can introduce their classroom friends.

4. Design bulletin boards that show personal similarities (hands, feet, nose, etc.) and differences (hair color, glasses, hearing aids, height, etc.)

5. Have a family project – send home bound blank books where families can collaborate and compose an "I Am Special Book" including photos and quotes from family members about the student.

6. Students use paper plates for their head shape, decorate with yarn, cloth, attach the "head" to a dowel and put at seats. Others try to identify who's who in their class. Use at open houses for parents to find their child.

7. Have a "Top Banana" bulletin board. Each Friday, draw a name out of the hat. That child becomes top banana for the week and decorates the bulletin board with any personal memorabilia – pictures, stuffed animals, baseball cards. Other classmates dictate positive statements about the top banana, which are written on cutout bananas to decorate the board.

8. Develop a birthday book. Children receive a page to write and illustrate – Happy Birthday! I like you because _____.

9. Adapt chores so included children can participate. Sew a piece of velcro to a mitten and attach a matching piece to an eraser so all children can erase the chalkboard.

10. Develop group names to encourage the feeling of belonging among peers. On one wing, which is called Candy Avenue, one class is the Peppermint Room, another the Lollipop Room and yet another the Lifesaver Room.

11. Note individual children's interests and send them personal postcards. ("Dear John, did you see the Phillies hit a home run last night? I thought of you." Or, "Dear Aimee, I noticed how you helped Ryan with his math homework this week. What a helper!")

A Letter From Denise

Regular educators may find ourselves so nervous and anxious about the return of differently-abled children to our classrooms and neighborhood schools that we wrongfully assume that the children are eager to be included. This letter will help to explain the anxiousness through the eyes of a child who has been in the special education setting.

Dear Mrs. Keener,

I am writing this letter with the help of Mrs. Robbins, my teacher. I am telling her what to write so you can read it. I have gone to Mrs. Robbins' class for five years. Her room is all the way down at the end of the big hall. I spend almost all day with Mrs. Robbins. I get to go to a class with smarter kids for lunch, singing, gym, library, and art. But those kids don't really know me. Ask them about me and they'll say, "Oh, Denise, she comes and goes, but she's not really one of us."

My teacher told me that this year I get to come to your room all day so I can make friends and learn with normal kids. It is going to be good for me, she says, but I am really, really scared.

Mrs. Robbins told me every day in school that I am good at things and I can learn. Will you think that? Will the smart kids have time to wait for me to finish my work?

For five years Mrs. Robbins has been teaching me in different ways. She reads me my school books or has them on tape. She reads tests to me and cuts them apart so they are short. She lets me do picture writing in my journal. Mrs. Robbins puts boxes around the problems I have to do in math so I don't have to look at the rest of the page. She gives me counters and calculators. Sometimes she folds papers like fans so I only do a piece at a time.

Mrs. Robbins worked hard to make learning easier for me. Will you do the same? I know Mrs. Robbins will come to your room sometimes to help me. She says she'll help you, too. Who will help me make friends? Will you talk slowly enough? Will the kids laugh at me?

I know you might say you don't have time to fix my learning, but please try. I know you are scared about having a different kind of kid in your class. I'm scared too. Please help me do a good job. Mrs. Robbins tells me I can learn and I can do it. Will you do the same for me?

Your friend,
Denise McIlwain

C: COOPERATION

Children are eager to come to school when involved in cooperative learning. They relate to the motto "None of us is as smart as all of us."

Teachers model and provide guided practice in cooperative learning, which is much more than counting off by fours and discussing George Washington.

Teachers need to clearly define group expectations and the role of each group member in the learning process. Children should be grouped to encompass diverse learning styles and can be reassigned every week or two, depending on the desired outcome.

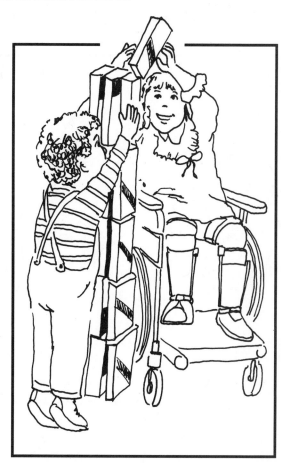

As children begin to work together and strive towards common goals, competitiveness will become obsolete. "I" will be spelled "W-E."

Cooperative learning has been shown to lessen disruptive behavior, increase appreciation of various abilities, promote positive self-esteem, and develop appropriate social interactions in the inclusive classroom.

Cooperative Groups Activity

Purpose:

To provide a variety of ways to set up cooperative groups.

Procedure:

As children enter the classroom the teacher pats each one on the back to say "Good Morning" and affixes a colored dot to each child's back. Children work together to find three other dots that are the same as theirs.

Paste six colorful magazine pictures on oak tag. Cut each picture into four puzzle pieces. Place one piece on each child's desk. Children must put four puzzles together to make their group.

Colored clothespins are placed on each child's desk. Children get into groups by matching clothespin colors.

Set up teams by word families. Individual children are given cards that say "at," "it," "op,""et," and "en." Those students need to find peers who are holding consonants to make appropriate words and form their team (s + it, b + it, h + it, and f + it).

These strategies ensure that ability levels are evenly distributed and all are included. Once children are in their groups, each member needs a participatory role. A special needs student in a cooperative group can act as the timekeeper (turns over a three-minute sand timer), the material distributor, notetaker (uses written language or picture cards to record team responses), the facilitator (keeps the group on task and is in charge of warm fuzzies), or the spokesperson (shares group report or consensus).

Children can wear a role card to remind themselves and each other of their job responsibilities. On the card list their job, their responsibility to the group, and sample statements used in that role. Teachers need to monitor groups to make sure that classmates do not take over the designated role from the differently-abled in their quest to help. All students must contribute equally toward group goals.

After group time children need time to reflect on the experience. Teachers can ask question such as, "Carmen, tell me three ways Rachel helped your team meet its goals," or, "Micha, what can you do tomorrow to help your team succeed?"

Children must be held accountable for their group performance. Teachers can circulate throughout the room with a checklist for monitoring performance. They can collect individual reports or group and individual assessments.

33 Ways to Applaud Your Teammates

1. "Wow!"
2. "Nice work!"
3. "You did it!"
4. "Thanks to you, we did it."
5. "Way to go!"
6. "Awesome Work!"
7. "Give me a high five."
8. "Good job."
9. "Neat-o!"
10. "Fantastic group work."
11. "Unbelievable."
12. "Now you're talking."
13. "Keep it going."
14. "We're so proud of you."
15. "You can do it."
16. "You're on the right track."
17. "Say it again so everyone can hear."
18. "Terrific timing!"
19. "First class job!"
20. "World class performance."
21. "Priceless performance."
22. "Cracker Jack kid."
23. "Sensational!"
24. "You're the cream of the crop."
25. "Astonishing contribution."
26. "Out of sight."
27. "We need your help."
28. "Marvelous music we make as a team."
29. "Spectacular."
30. "Thrilling."
31. "Let's shake on it."
32. "Here's looking at you."
33. "You put this smile on my face."

33 Ways to Encourage Your Teammates

1. "Let's look at this again."
2. "May I show you how?"
3. "Try it another time."
4. "Let's do it together."
5. "I think this may help."
6. "Remember when . . . "
7. "Try it this way."
8. "This stuff was hard, wasn't it?"
9. "Tell me more about this answer."
10. "Maybe this picture clue will help."
11. "Let's try another guess."
12. "Almost . . . "
13. "I tried it this way."
14. "This part looks great."
15. "Don't give up."
16. "You are really working hard."
17. "Think again."
18. "I know you can do it."
19. "Are you sure?"
20. "Do you want to give it more thought?"
21. "Please do what you can."
22. "Let's tackle it together."
23. "Go for it."
24. "Together we can make an attempt."
25. "Give it all you've got."
26. "Take another crack at this."
27. "Close . . ."
28. "I'll bet you can."
29. "Let us give you a hand."
30. "Tell me more."
31. "We are all pulling for you."
32. "We did something like this before."
33. "You might try this approach."

D: DIVERSITY

Inclusion does not overlook diversities, but welcomes the vast array of student needs in the classroom. Teachers need to show children how to constructively discuss differences and learn from one another.

Appearances aren't always what they seem to be. As vital as differences are, children need to avoid misconceptions about outward appearances. Simply because a child is in a wheelchair shouldn't prevent him or her from participating in classroom activities.

"Inclusion does not overlook diversities, but welcomes the vast array of student needs in the classroom."

illustration
by Jonathan Eshenour

Diversity Tips

1. Pair all students for job chart. This way no one is singled out for needing extra assistance.

2. Encourage small group work on classroom projects. (Jonathan may not be able to write a report on Native Americans, but he is able to make a clay figure for Keith's report.)

3. Allow for playtime and socializing within the classroom. Regardless of their ages, all elementary children need time to play.

4. Review balloons used in the acceptance section to encourage group discussions about diversity.

5. Use role playing, dramatizations, collages, and journal writing to help promote an awareness and acceptance of diversity.

6. Develop thematic lessons around diversity.

Activity Ideas

1. Share Mario Mariotti's *Hanimals and Humages*. These colorful books allow children's imaginations to blossom while at the same time bringing awareness of human diversities. Children quickly respond to the similarities in pictures of body features such as hands, feet, and faces which quickly change with the application of paint.

Trace students' hands. Allow them to decorate cutout hands in creative ways. Use stage make-up and have children turn hands into hanimals. Photograph the individual hanimals and display in the room.

2. Write a class book titled *"If I Could Change One Thing about Myself . . . "*

3. Develop "I Am So Board" day once a month. Children bring their favorite board game to school. The class is divided into groups of 3-4 students. One child in each group must explain the game directions to others. Children play the game for 15-20 minutes. At the end of that time, a different group member teaches another game.

4. Encourage children to coauthor stories during writing time. Possibilities include: a child who is not a fluent writer can dictate a story to a partner; a topic can be decided upon jointly and children can web or outline and write the story together; one child writes the story and another child who has difficulty writing illustrates it.

5. Bulletin boards can display pictures of individual play preferences at home, at recess, or in classrooms. Examples are shown of home similarities, a variety of holidays, or clothing.

Diversity Activity

Purpose:

To validate the feeling that each individual is unique and special although like others in many ways.

Procedure:

Introduce children to *People* by Spier.

People by Peter Spier

This book provides a multitude of differences and similarities young children can easily grasp.

Photograph each child in the class and enlarge photos to 5-by-7 inches. Cut out masks to place over the photo so just the eyes are visible. Hang the "Eyes Have It" on a bulletin board. Have children attempt to match names to eyes as a center activity.

Make silhouette pictures of children. Shine a filmstrip light on the profile of a child sitting in front of a wall. Trace the child's outline on bright paper. Mount on black backgrounds and have classmates identify children by their profiles.

Have children cut large facial pictures out of magazines. Fold the picture in half and cut on the fold. Glue one-half of the face on paper. Have children draw the missing half on the paper. This activity stresses symmetry, facial characteristics, and differences among individual projects.

Invite families to help children make a collage of photographs depicting "Things My Family Likes." Display collages, noticing familial diversity in enjoyment.

Encourage cultural diversity within the classroom by having parents discuss particular family customs.

Color Hunt

This activity can sensitize primary-grade children to similarities and differences within the classroom. Children fill in the first column with the color of their eyes, hair, etc., then find and write the name of a classmate with the same color listed for each category.

1. eyes   _____   _____

2. hair   _____   _____

3. bike   _____   _____

4. car   _____   _____

5. house   _____   _____

6. shoes   _____   _____

7. bedroom   _____   _____

8. pants   _____   _____

9. socks   _____   _____

10. shirt   _____   _____

Diversities that May Be Present in the Regular Education Setting

Social:
- unable to partake in social play
- unable to play alone or with others
- unable to share
- unaware of feelings of others
- lack knowledge of world other than their own
- unaware of need for food, clothing, shelter
- unaware of likenesses and differences in children
- lack understanding of behavior and consequences
- unable to be a follower and a leader
- lack close friendships
- unaware of social and familial relationships
- unable to express appropriate emotions and feelings

Academic:
- unable to learn from play
- lack experiences to build on academically
- unable to use language to relate to experience
- unable to correlate written and spoken language
- lack interest in a variety of learning situations
- lack experience of hearing appropriate literature
- unaware of age-appropriate vocabulary
- lack ability to organize material
- lack interest in mathematical functions
- unaware of numeration
- lack foundation for developing reading, writing skills
- unable to correlate environment to learning experiences
- lack independent learning skills

Physical:
- unable to move and manipulate objects
- unable to visually focus on objects

- lack age-appropriate eye-hand coordination
- unable to identify body parts
- lack awareness of physical limitations and abilities
- inconsistent age-appropriate growth and development
- inability to stand, walk, climb, balance, gallop, run, or skip
- difficulty with fine motor skills
- difficulty with gross motor skills
- unable to sit for long periods
- lack interest in physical activities

Environmental:
- homeless children
- migrant children
- crack babies
- step families
- incarcerated parents
- foster children
- adoptive families
- special needs siblings
- grandparents with custody
- children of alcoholics
- drugs in the home
- child abuse
- racial differences
- gender awareness
- religious and cultural diversity

All students can learn and succeed but not on the same day in the same way.

The key is expanded opportunity and support for learning success.

Children in the Classroom Are More Alike Than Different

Typical Child   **All Children**   **Special Needs Child**

Special Needs Child

May require assistive devices

Individualized Educational Program in place

May require support personnel to achieve IEP goals

May require adaptive furniture or more classroom space

May require longer "think time"

May require flexible schedules

May require more understanding, empathy

May present physical challenges

May require assistance with relevance of learning

All Children

Represent knowledge in a variety of ways

Self-esteem relates to ability to learn

Learn through individual style

Learn through play

Accept differences as norm

Curious learners

Development dependent on social interactions

Need to belong to classroom community and feel membership

Need to develop lifelong skills

Friendships necessary both during and after school

Recognition is needed for individual gifts/talents

Need to become independent thinkers

Enjoy cooperative learning, peer tutors, cross-age tutors

Respond well to active learning and learning centers

Need to represent learning in a variety of channels

Need cooperative effort of home/school

Wide range of individual needs

Learn by doing

Typical Child

May be more independent

Able to verbalize wants and needs through language

Easily accepted in society

Aware of own strengths and limitations

Often uses all sensory channels

Has power to use learning

Self-directed learner

E: EVOLUTION OF EXCELLENCE

The evolution of inclusion is a gradual process. Be wary if you are informed that "Tomorrow we'll begin inclusion." Keep in mind that the foundation for excellence must be in place before the project can be successful. Preparation is crucial for success.

Regardless of careful preparation done ahead of time, there may be educators who will resist this change, close their doors and hope this will go away. While some teachers will never change, others will watch the process evolve and have their fears diminished as they see and hear from colleagues about the success stories blossoming in their classrooms.

Some teachers will say, "I saw your kids smiling, tell me more"; some will say, "I'd like help developing a health lesson for different levels"; and others will begin requesting to have differently-abled children in their class.

The entire evolutionary process may take up to five years for successful completion. In the beginning, administrators may carefully place children in classrooms of the most positive, caring staff because they know that success breeds success.

"The entire evolutionary process may take up to five years for successful completion."

Evolution of Excellence Tips

1. Have a task force in place prior to becoming inclusionary. Districts that involve administrators, teachers with a variety of expertise, community members, PTO members, and parents as part of building-based teams will have the necessary "champions of children" ready to facilitate inclusion before the children arrive. The task force can develop the vision for inclusion, determine steps needed to reach goals, and define individual responsibilities.

2. Invite children to share their feelings about friendships with included students at PTO meetings or Back to School meetings. Children can express their personal success stories and answer questions honestly.

3. Inclusive schools demonstrate their commitment to the education of all children through a district mission statement and practices that support it. Once adopted by the Board of Education a mission statement becomes the driving force behind an equitable education for all children.

    A sample mission statement might look like this: The "Anyplace School District" believes that all students are capable of learning and being successful. Our district mission is to provide a quality education for all students; to promote academic, social, and personal excellence; and to foster the development of responsible citizenship. This mission is a joint effort of our community, parents, staff and students.

4. Before inclusion begins, make sure support systems are in place for students and staff so no one feels alone. Teachers must be able to work as part of a team and be comfortable collaborating with colleagues.

5. All staff, including custodians, cafeteria workers, secretaries, administrators, teachers, counselors, instructional assistants, bus drivers, and nurses need to be made aware of the philosophy of inclusion and how it affects their job description. Staff members should receive descriptions of the differently-abled children they will be in contact with and the proper procedures needed to ensure success for that child.

    I remember one bus driver thinking that he was doing 7-year-old Marsha a favor by carrying her into her classroom each day. What she really needed was to become comfortable with her walker and join her peers in the hallway. We had forgotten to include him in team meetings to set Marsha's educational and social goals. As soon as he was part of the collaborative team, Marsha walked to her class.

Five-Year Plan for Inclusion

Elementary Schedule - Year 1

	Day 1	Day 2	Day 3	Day 4	Day 5	Day 6
9:00 - 9:40	----------------Opening, Calendar, Bathroom, Support as Needed----------					
9:45 - 10:25						
10:30 - 11:10						
11:15 - 11:55						
12:00 - 12:40	LUNCH	LUNCH	LUNCH	LUNCH	LUNCH	LUNCH
12:45 - 1:20						
1:25 - 2:05						
2:10 - 2:50						

During the first year the students would be with regular education students where written. Blank areas represent time for pull-out programs.

Elementary Schedule - Year 2

	Day 1	Day 2	Day 3	Day 4	Day 5	Day 6
9:00 - 9:40	----------------Opening, Calendar, Bathroom, Support as Needed----------					
9:45 - 10:25						
10:30 - 11:10						
11:15 - 11:55						
12:00 - 12:40	LUNCH	LUNCH	LUNCH	LUNCH	LUNCH	LUNCH
12:45 - 1:20	Prep Period	Team Meetings	Planning	Collaboration	Planning	Planning
1:25 - 2:05						
2:10 - 2:50						

Time provided for collaboration and planning.

Elementary Schedule - Year 3

	Day 1	Day 2	Day 3	Day 4	Day 5	Day 6
9:00 - 9:40	---------------Opening, Calendar, Bathroom, Support as Needed--------------					
9:45 - 10:25						
10:30 - 11:10						
11:15 - 11:55						
12:00 - 12:40	-------------------------------------LUNCH----------------------------------					
12:45 - 1:20	Prep Period	Team Meetings	Planning	Collaboration	Planning	Planning
1:25 - 2:05	----------------------------Handwriting Support as Requested----------------------------					
2:10 - 2:50	Thematic Units	Cooperative	Groups	Peer Tutors	Volunteers	Volunteers

Children included for handwriting and thematic units.

Elementary Schedule - Year 4

	Day 1	Day 2	Day 3	Day 4	Day 5	Day 6
9:00 - 9:40	---------------Opening, Calendar, Bathroom, Support as Needed----------					
9:45 - 10:25						
10:30 - 11:10						
11:15 - 11:55	Math Room # 17, 31 TA 23, 24		Math Room #23, 24 TA 17, 31	Math Room #23, 24 TA 17, 31	Monitoring	
12:00 - 12:40	---------------------------------------LUNCH----------------------------------					
12:45 - 1:20	Prep Period	Team Meetings	Planning	Collaboration	Planning	Planning
1:25 - 2:05	----------------------------Handwriting Support as Requested----------------------------					
2:10 - 2:50	Thematic Units	Cooperative	Groups	Peer Tutors	Volunteers	Volunteers

Classrooms with TA represent times when a teaching assistant is in the classroom. Classrooms without TA marked represent times with a special education support teacher in that room. Blank areas are pull-out times.

Elementary Schedule - Year 5

	Day 1	Day 2	Day 3	Day 4	Day 5	Day 6
9:00 - 9:40	---------------Opening, Calendar, Bathroom, Support as Needed----------------					
9:45 - 10:25	-----------------------------------Language Arts-----------------------------------					
	Room # 23, 24, 31	Room #17	Room #17	Room # 23, 24, 31	Room #23, 24 pull out/ resource room	
10:30 - 11:10	-----------------------------------Language Arts-----------------------------------					
	Room #17 TA	Room # 23, 24, 32	Room # 23, 24, 31	Room # 17	Room 17, 31 pullout/ resource room	
11:15 - 11:55	Math Room # 17, 31 TA 23, 24		Math Room # 23, 24 TA 17, 31	Math Room # 23, 24 TA 17, 31	Monitoring	
12:00 - 12:40	-------------------------------------- LUNCH--					
12:45 - 1:20	Prep Period	Team Meetings	Planning	Collaboration	Planning	Planning
1:25 - 2:05	----------------------------Handwriting Support as Requested---------------------------					
2:10 - 2:50	Thematic Units	Cooperative	Groups	Peer Tutors	Volunteers	Volunteers

Add language arts with teaching assistant and support teacher in classroom.
Allow times for pull out as needed by students.

Primary Grades Special Education Support Schedule

18 students, 4 classes

1 teaching assistant (TA) and 1 special education teacher

	Monday	Tuesday	Wednesday	Thursday	Friday
8:00 - 8:30	-------------------- HOME ROOM/OPENING ACTIVITIES------------------------				
8:30 - 9:00	JOURNAL Room 2-TA Room 1	Room 1-TA Room 2	Room 1 Room 2-TA	Room 1-TA Room 2	MATH Room 10 Room 12-TA
9:00 - 10:30	L ARTS Room 2 Room 1-TA	Room 2-TA Room 1	Room 1-TA Room 2	Room 1 Room 2-TA	MATH Room 12 Room 10-TA
10:30 - 11:10	MATH Room 2-TA Room 1	Room 2 Room 1-TA	Room 2-TA Room 1	Room 2 Room 1-TA	THEMES Room 12 Room 10-TA
11:15 - 12:15	Lunch/ Collaborate Tutor Room 10-TA	Room 10-TA	Room 10-TA	Room 12-TA	Room 12-TA
12:15 - 12:45	MATH Room 2 Lunch -TA	Room 1	Room 2	Room 1	Room 2
12:45 - 1:05	PULL OUT/TUTOR-- Room 2-TA				
1:05 - 1:50	L ARTS Room 12-TA Room 10	Room 12 Room 10-TA	Room 10 Room 12-TA	Room 10-TA Room 12	THEMES Room 2-TA Room 1
1:50 - 2:15	L ARTS Room 10-TA Room 12	Room 12-TA Room 10	Room 12 Room 10-TA	Room 10 Room 12-TA	THEMES Room 2 Room 1-TA
2:15 - 3:05	---Team Meetings---				
3:05 - 3:45	-----------------Prepare Materials, Observe, General Support-----------------------				

TA = Teaching Assistant

Rooms without "TA" signify support staff in.

Intermediate Grades Special Education Support Schedule

12 students, 4 classrooms
1 special education teacher, parent volunteer

	Monday	Tuesday	Wednesday	Thursday	Friday
8:00 - 8:30	------------------------------------ TEAM MEETINGS------------------------------				
8:30 - 9:00	Math (Mrs. H.)	Math (Mr. J.)	Math (Mrs. H.)	Math (Mr. J)	Math (J or H)
9:00 - 10:30	English (Mrs. T) Reading (Mrs. A)	English (Mrs. T)	Reading (Mrs. A)	English (Mrs. T)	Reading (Mrs. A)
10:30 - 11:10	Lang - Arts (Mr. J or Mrs. H)	Reading (Mrs. H)	Lang - Arts (Mr. J) (Mrs. H)	Lang - Arts (Mr. J) (Mrs. T)	Lang - Arts (Mr. J) (Mrs. H)
11:15 - 12:15	------------------------------- LUNCH/COLLABORATION------------------------------				
	(Mrs. H) (Mr. J)	(Mrs. T)	(Mrs. A)	(Mrs. T)	(Mrs. T) (Mrs. H)
12:15 - 12:45	Reading (Mrs. H)	Reading (Mrs. H)	Reading (Mrs. T)	Reading (Mrs. T)	Reading (Mrs. T)
12:45 - 1:05	---------------------------------------Math--				
			(Mrs. A)		
1:05 - 1:50	Lang - Arts (Mr. J)	Lang - Arts (Mr. J) (Mrs. T)	Lang - Arts (Mr. J) (Mrs. T)	Lang -Arts (Mr. J) (Mrs. T)	Tutor Time
1:50 - 2:15	Reading (Mrs. T)	Reading (Mrs. T)	Spelling (Mrs. A)	Soc. St/Sci (Mrs. H)	Tutor Time
2:15 - 3:05	Soc. St/Sci (Mrs. T)	Soc. St/Sci (Mrs. A)	Soc. St/Sci (Mr. J)	HOBBY CLUB	Tutor Time
3:05 - 3:45	----------------------------------Prep Time, Meetings-----------------------------				

Fitting the Pieces Together . . .

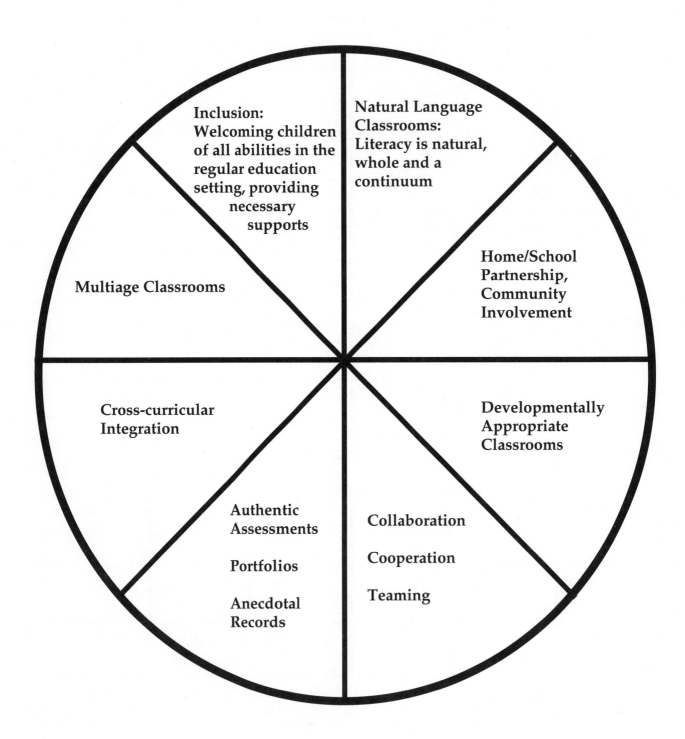

Inclusion is one piece of the puzzle in restructuring schools.
Without all the pieces in place, a fragmented picture will result.

The Inclusion Change Process

Successful Inclusion	Confusion	Anxious, Frightened	Slow Change	Frustrated, Over-worked	False Starts
=	=	=	=	=	=
Action Plan: Who Does What, When	Action Plan: Who Does What, When	Action Plan: Who Does What, When	Action Plan: Who Does What, When	Action Plan: Who Does What, When	
+	+	+	+	+	+
Materials, Resources, In-class Support	Materials, Resources, In-class Support	Materials, Resources, In-class Support	Materials, Resources, In-class Support		Materials, Resources, In-class Support
+	+	+	+	+	+
Shared Philosophy & Teaming	Shared Philosophy & Teaming	Shared Philosophy & Teaming		Shared Philosophy & Teaming	Shared Philosophy & Teaming
+	+	+	+	+	+
Inservice Staff	Inservice Staff		Inservice Staff	Inservice Staff	Inservice Staff
+	+	+	+	+	+
Mission Statement District Support		Mission Statement District Support	Mission Statement District Support	Mission Statement District Support	Mission Statement District Support

F: FRIENDSHIP

Developing and maintaining friendships is the cornerstone of a truly accepting inclusive classroom. The theme of making friends and being a friend should be woven throughout the established curriculum rather then being an isolated "subject area."

A caring classroom embraces the philosophy that children are unique and totally individual. It adapts to children's learning channels and interests and encourages children to be aware of others' needs.

Teachers can help children connect personal life experiences to their school life. They can also encourage parents to cultivate their children's after-school interactions with differently-abled youngsters. By allowing parents an active role within the classroom they can observe the budding relationships and assist children with extending their friendships.

illustration
by Jennifer Cary

It is the responsibility of schools and society to help all children develop self-confidence and friendships. The friendships we help foster within our classrooms today can shape the future of tomorrow's communities.

Friendship Tips

1. Share traditional family holiday treats. Children bring in recipes, write a class cookbook, have an in-class tasting party, measure ingredients, discuss scientific principles of before/after cooking, and share treats at a local nursing home.

2. Set classroom desks in neighborhoods and groups rather than in rows.

3. Develop student interest surveys to increase individualization and forming friends (see page 45).

4. Allow time daily to greet students personally and set a friendly tone.

5. Develop a classroom directory to help parents cultivate after-school interactions with differently-abled children (see page 46). Include all children in socializing possibilities.

6. Use circle time to encourage a feeling of togetherness and to develop active listening skills.

Circle of Friends Activity

A classroom teacher or instructional consultant talks with children about a new student who may be coming into the classroom. The facilitator shares general information regarding the student, name, needs, and fears. Open discussion encourages classmates to welcome the student into their Circle of Friends.

After the discussion, students receives a blackline master (see next page) of four concentric circles with a figure which represents them in the middle.

Beginning with the inner circle, students put dots to represent people (or pets) they love the most.

The dots placed in the second circle represent a student's best friends.

In the third circle, children place dots to represent acquaintances they may do things with, but who are not their best friends.

The dots in the outside circle represent those people who are paid for services performed in the student's life. (Doctor, dentist, dance instructor, etc.)

The facilitator invites children to share the number of dots placed in each circle and places dots on an overhead to represent a range of student responses.

Following a discussion, the facilitator places circle completed by an imaginary friend on the overhead. This circle may have a dad and a dog in the inner circle and five paid medical assistants in the outer circle. Children share their answers to "How would you feel if this was you?"

Children are encouraged to discuss why we all need friends and how to work together so the new student's circle does not resemble the imaginary one.

This activity can be repeated throughout the year to encourage students to develop a variety of in-class friendships.

Purpose:

This activity helps children understand that friendship is a two-way street and allows for empathic discussion about friends and feelings.

Procedure:

The teacher or consultant should become familiar with the Circle of Friends activity developed by Judith Snow and Marsha Forest in *Educating All Students in the Mainstream of Regular Education*, 1987 (see professional bibliography, pages 193-194).

Circle of Friends Activity

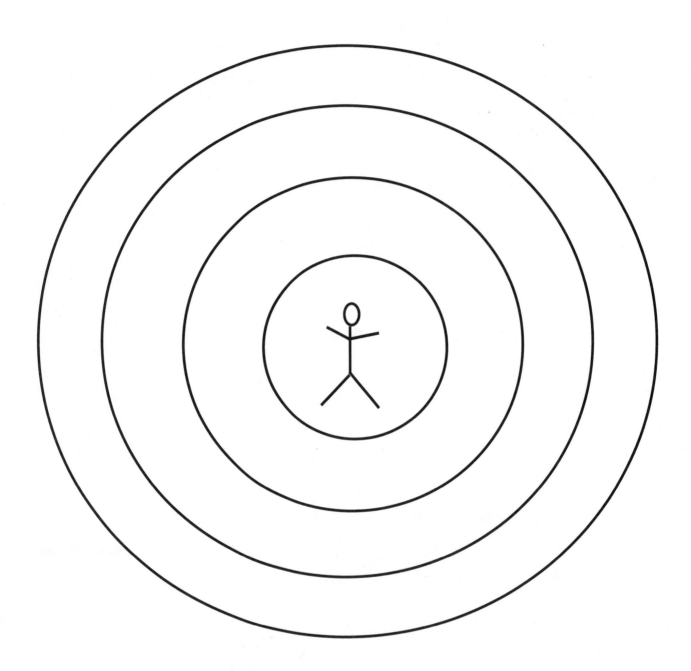

Student Interest Survey

This form can be used with primary children in September and read to nonreaders. It lends itself to individualizing projects and forming friends based on interests or hobbies.

1. My full name is_____

2. My pets are_____

3. My favorite TV show is_____

4. My favorite food is_____

5. What I like to do outside_____

6. What I like to do inside_____

7. It is easy for me to_____

8. It is hard for me to_____

9. My favorite story (or author) is_____

10. I am happy when_____

11. I am sad when_____

12. I am really good at _____

Classroom Directory

In order to promote after-school socialization, many teachers develop a classroom directory. The directory assists parents with inviting friends home after school, provides directions to homes from a common starting point, and encourages children to match names with faces they see each day in school. Teachers can help parents understand the value in this directory and obtain permission from them to include student photos. Parents who hesitate to have their child's photo in the book will often allow the child to include a self-portrait.

DIRECTORY OF ROOM 10 FRIENDS

(Place an individual picture here.)

Hi! My name is:

_____

My phone number is:

_____

I live with:

_____
(Name of primary caregiver)

My address is:

_____

If you want to get to my house from this school, here are the directions:

_____

_____

_____

Parent permission:

_____

G: GIFTS OF ALL

Every child has a special gift to share. Often we define "the gifted/talented child" as one who has a high IQ. This shortsightedness may make classroom teachers unaware of gifts other children have.

Educator Priscilla Vail (1987) says, "as each child is a gift, so each child comes with distinguishing gifts." Children demonstrate their talent and natural ability in a variety of degrees. Teachers who integrate children in the regular classroom setting learn to recognize all students' gifts and talents and provide educational challenges to meet

their needs. One child's giftedness may be explaining Plato's philosophies or how the moon affects the tide. But what about the gifts bestowed upon you by the child who is able, at last, to locate the classroom on his or her own? Or how about the child who is finally able to make eye contact with another person?

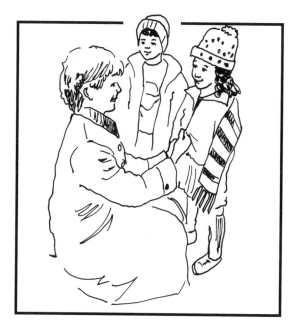

As children learn to recognize and appreciate the gifts and talents of peers, they will become more comfortable and secure with recognizing their own giftedness.

Classroom Milestones Book

To applaud individual milestones during the school year.

Procedure:

Each child is given a small composition book. The front is decorated and personalized by the child to make a "My Classroom Milestones" book.

Throughout the school year, the child records individual milestones reached and the date of its accomplishment at the top of the page. The child then illustrates the page, cuts out a magazine picture to represent the milestone, or has a Polaroid picture placed on the page.

Sample milestones may include: read my first trade book – 9/29, edited my first process writing book – 10/11, memorized addition facts to 10 – 11/18, ate lunch unassisted – 11/14, used the bathroom unassisted – 9/25, made eye contact for two minutes – 2/18.

Classroom Yellow Pages Directory

Xerox on yellow paper and bind into one book. Title the book as a "Directory of Helpers in Room _____," or "Our Yellow Pages."

Encourage children to place their name on the pages where they are capable of completing the task. Place social, behavioral, and academic skills throughout the book.

The Yellow Pages should provide opportunities for all children to sign up on a number of pages.

Children use each other as resources when help is needed. If Johnny can't zip his coat and the class is lined up for recess, the teacher invites him to get out the Yellow Pages and ask someone who signed up to help with zipping.

Purpose:

To develop a classroom directory listing individual strengths and talents.

Procedure:

Use simple academic and nonacademic skills and graphics for each page of the "Yellow Pages." (See samples on this page and the next page. Cut apart and use as page headings.)

Classroom Yellow Pages . . .
A Directory of Helpers in Our Room

Let's learn letters together.

Let's build together.

I will help you play a game.

I will be your friend at free time.

I like to help clean up.

I will help you cut.

Call on me when you need help.

I like to write.

I can help get your supplies.

I will help you count.

I will help you pack to go home.

I will help you tie shoes.

I will book share with you.

I will help you catch a ball.

I will teach you your phone number.

I will help you learn your address.

I can help you zip or snap.

H: HELPING EACH OTHER

Children helping children is the norm in an inclusive classroom. One method of encouraging helpmates is cooperative learning, which was explained in an earlier section. In addition to eliminating competition, cooperative learning challenges children to excel and achieve their own level of excellence while eagerly helping each other obtain team goals.

Children can learn the art of helping, including how not to "over help."

Helping Each Other Tips

1. Assign children a study buddy to help review assignments, set up listening centers, coauthor books, organize homework, and provide phone reminders such as "Remember your permission slip for the zoo tomorrow!" or "Ryan needs to bring in two potatoes for our stone soup project on Friday."

2. Pair children for book sharing. One child reads aloud a trade book while the other partner listens to the story. Children can check each other for understanding by asking questions, pointing to pictures for a review of facts, or assembling sentence strips from the story in the correct order.

3. Peers can remind each other when it's time to visit a nurse for medication or when it's time for a bathroom break. A picture of a clock could be taped to children's desks with hands showing the correct time for their job. This responsibility can be assigned on a weekly basis.

4. Children can help each other accomplish life-skills IEP goals in grocery stores, post offices, or department stores.

5. Establish a welcome wagon committee in each classroom. Every month form a new committee of four to six students. These students are given brown grocery bags, glitter, glue, ribbon, and metallic paper. The children write on the bag "Welcome to Room _____." Inside the bags the team places pencils, pens, markers, glue, scissors, and necessary books. As a new student comes into the classroom, the committee greets the child, presents this "gift bag," and helps make the newcomer's transition to class smoother. Not only does this relieve stress on the teacher, but it also helps children take ownership for what happens in their classroom.

6. Give all children a two-sided sign (Please help me/Keep working, I'm OK). Signs are displayed on the desk as help is needed.

7. Glue a red and green one-inch cube together. When working independently on a project, a child turns the block to show his/her need for help (green cube up = keep moving, red cube up = stop to help me).

8. Develop a helping chain to hang. Cut out chain strips (1" x 4 ½"). When one child has been helped by another and wants to show public appreciation, the child writes the name of the helper on the strip and hooks it onto the helping friends chain. It will soon outgrow your classroom.

9. Discuss children's literature such as *The Piggybook* by Anthony Browne.

10. Select groups of children may be assigned to help physically challenged students exit for a fire drill or carry lunch trays as needed.

Wheelchair Safety

To teach children how to safely operate a wheelchair for another child.

 Small groups of four to six children are taken to a spacious area to work. (Blacktop, gym, all-purpose room)

Safety pylons are set up in an obstacle course fashion. Empty wheelchairs are brought into the area.

Children first learn how to put the brakes on and off on the wheelchair.

Children practice pushing the wheelchairs between the pylons, taking careful corners and smooth turns.

Children are taken outside to practice going up and down curbs while pushing a wheelchair.

Children receive instruction on how to safely push a wheelchair up and down a ramp.

Children now receive a wheelchair buddy and officially practice taking that friend for a practice ride through the school.

After completion of this training course, (approximately two to three days) the newly trained drivers receive an official wheelchair driver's license.

The licenses are proudly displayed when driving friends throughout the school or on the playground.

illustration by Jennifer Cary

This is to certify that

_____

has successfully completed a
Wheelchair Safety course
on this _____ day of _____.

You have shown us that you are
responsible and considerate
of others.

Thank you!

Peer Tutoring Program

Send a tutoring program letter to interested classes (see next page).

Purpose:

To develop a peer tutoring program to help children meet specific classroom goals and increase individual accountability.

Procedure:

Team each primary classroom with an intermediate classroom to develop cross-age tutors.

Invite a current tutor to speak to interested classrooms and describe his or her tutoring responsibilities.

Send a tutoring program letter to interested classes (see next page).

Schedule tutors to come to classes during their noninstructional time.

Classroom teachers meet with tutors for training sessions to establish rules, expectations, and accountability.

Tutoring Program Invitation Letter

This is an informational letter sent in the beginning of the year to make students and parents aware of the peer tutoring program.

TUTORING PROGRAM

Dear 4th and 5th Graders:

We are ready to begin another year of tutoring with primary children in grades K, 1 and 2, and we need your help! Many of the children need a buddy to read to them, listen to them read, or help them complete work.

If you are interested in helping your little friends do well in school, you need to have a parent and homebase teacher sign this form.

You will be assigned a noninstructional time to come into a primary classroom (before school, study hall, recess). The teacher you will be working with will contact you for your first training session. After you meet your pal, your tutoring will begin.

Thanks for your help!

Sincerely,

- -

The best time for_____ to tutor

and not miss instruction is_____.

_____
Homebase Teacher

My child has permission to become part of a school-wide tutoring club.

_____
Parent or Guardian

Letter to Volunteer Tutors

Teachers can use a form like this to develop training and scheduling for cross-age tutoring.

TO:

HOMEROOM:

GRADE:

CONGRATULATIONS!!

You will be coming to Grade_____, Room #_____
to begin tutoring with_____.

Your first training session will be held on _____ and
you will meet your buddy after that meeting.
I appreciate your help and know that this experience will
help you both become better students and better people.

Your homebase teacher and family will be informed of
your hard work.

I look forward to meeting with you.

Sincerely,

I: Individualized Education Program/Plan (IEP)

In 1975 the United States Congress passed Public Law 94-142, the Education for All Handicapped Children Act. This law requires that all states establish procedures that ensure "that to the maximum extent appropriate, handicapped children, including those children in public or private institutions or other care facilities, are educated with children who are not handicapped, and that special classes, separate schooling, or other removal of handicapped children from the regular educational environment occurs only when the nature or severity of the handicap is such that education in regular classes with the use of supplementary aides and services cannot be achieved satisfactorily."

In essence, PL 94-142 is the law which demands that students receive an education in the least restrictive environment (LRE). To ensure that identified students meet educational goals, federal law also mandates that such students have an Individualized Education Program (IEP) in place.

The IEP can be one of the most frightening aspects of inclusion for the regular education teacher. Many teachers have never seen an IEP, let alone been required to incorporate one into their teaching.

"The IEP can be one of the most frightening aspects of inclusion for the regular education teacher."

Traditionally, goals for a child's IEP are developed around the individual's strengths and needs. A team comprised of the child's parents or caregiver, school psychologist, instructional consultant, guidance counselor, building principal, special education supervisor, classroom teacher, support personnel (speech, occupational therapist, physical therapist, audiologist, etc.), special education teacher, and any other teachers who come in contact with the student during the school day collaborate to plan for the student's success. Many districts are beginning to include the special needs student and a peer in this meeting. (Typically this is done from age twelve and up). Data gathered from the student and peer is often invaluable.

Input for the IEP is initially developed from a parent survey (see page 62), which may incorporate questions on self-help, basic help, recreation and leisure activities, academic, social, and language skills. Woven throughout the team meeting for development of the IEP will be such phrases as "age-appropriate peers," "nondisabled peers," "in a typical classroom setting."

IEPs should reflect a distinct relationship between the existing curriculum and a child's needs. Special education jargon should be minimized so IEPs can be understood by all educators and parents. Members present at the IEP meeting should have a clear idea of the need for specially-designed instruction and the location of the delivery services.

IEP objectives should be obtainable within the classroom settings and address why the skill is important, where the learning will take place, what skills are necessary to obtain the goal, and how it will be obtained. The IEP should define the special service as a support, not a location.

A sample IEP goal might look like this: Aimee will be able to identify the one-to-one correspondence of numerals 1-10 while being integrated in an age-appropriate typical classroom. The materials to use are manipulatives, saltbox writing, and large writing utensils. Peer tutors and cooperative learning groups will be utilized as needed. The special education department will provide in-class support and consultation. (See page 185 for a sample IEP.)

"IEP objectives should be obtainable within the classroom settings . . ."

Best Practices in IEP Development

In order to implement an activity-based program in the daily classroom schedule you need to be able to answer the following questions:

1. Are the selected IEP goals, critical activities, and skills from the following domains: domestic, vocational, recreation/leisure, regular education curriculum?

2. Do the IEP goals/activities reflect the family's priorities and goals as stated in a parent inventory?

3. Do the IEP goals/activities reflect the student's preferences, interests, and needs?

4. Does the need for this IEP activity/goal occur frequently across multiple environments and within natural settings?

5. Does the IEP goal/activity promote inclusion and interdependence?

6. Would the task and materials be respected or used by his/her same-age peers?

7. Can you enhance or build upon an already existing skill/ability within the regular classroom?

8. Does it support "the principle of partial participation?" (creating adaptations which encourage students of varying abilities to participate at varying rates within the typical classroom and allow children to move out of the regular room if necessary)

9. Does the IEP include adaptive devices, strategies, and other supports?

10. Has the special education department explained the IEP to the regular education staff and clearly defined who is responsible for which portion?

IEP INVENTORY

Family members fill out the inventory prior to and share it in the IEP meeting. (See page 173 for a completed example.)

PARENT QUESTIONNAIRE

Student Name_____ Age_____

Parent Name_____

Address_____

_____

1. List three activities your child takes part in with your family.

    a._____

    b._____

    c._____

2. How extensively is your child involved in these activities?

3. Is your child able to entertain him/herself alone?

4. What recreational activities can be implemented at school to improve your child's quality of life?

5. List your child's three favorite stories

    a._____

    b._____

    c._____

6. What reading skills do you see as part of your child's educational plan (listening to stories, identifying story characters, recognizing simple words, sounding out words, reading words in context, recognizing words around the community)?

7. List three math skills your child demonstrates at home (one-to-one correspondence counting, value of money, making change, telling time, measuring, using a calculator, identifying numerals, writing numerals, adding and subtracting).

8. Using the examples from number seven, what math skills would you like to see your child acquire this year?

9. Describe your child's fine motor skills (button, snap, zip, stringing beads, using writing instruments, tie shoes, coloring, cutting, and pasting). How can the school improve these skills?

10. Describe your child's communication skills (speaks in sentences, phrases, or single words, uses sign language, noncommunicative, easily understood).

11. Is your child more comfortable communicating with certain family members or peers than others? Please describe.

12. Does your child maintain eye contact during communication?

13. Is your child able to follow oral directions? A two-step direction?

14. List three ways you'd like to see your child's language skills improved.

15. List three social activities you'd like your child to take part in.

16. Are there any other skills or activities not noted that you would like your child to learn?

17. List three ways you would like to be contacted regarding school information (phone, postcards, weekly diary).

Note: Many multiage schools use similar questions when discussing placements with parents. Children in a multiage setting may have individualized educational plans in place, regardless of exceptionality.

J: JARGON

The use of specialized jargon often impedes the inclusion process. Many times parents, children, and regular educators shake their heads in confusion as special educators, psychologists, and administrators speak in this foreign tongue. All educators must become familiar with the technical terms used or eliminate them until there is a universal language. Some schools have their special education department develop a list of their most commonly used terms. Such a list might look like this:

AA — Age-appropriate (placement by chronological rather than mental age)

AAC — Augmentative and alternative communication

ADD — Attention deficit disorder

BD — Behavioral disorder

CA — Chronological age

CBA — Curriculum-based assessment

CF — Cystic fibrosis

CP — Cerebral palsy

DD — Developmental disability

DS — Down Syndrome

EMR — Educable mentally retarded

ES — Emotional support

FAPE — Free appropriate public education

FC — Facilitated communication

HI — Hearing impaired

IDEA — Individuals with Disabilities Education Act

IEP - Individualized education program/plan

IFSP — Individualized family service plan

IST — Instructional support team/teacher

ITP — Individualized transition plan

LD — Learning disability/disabled

LRE — Least restrictive environment

LS — Learning support

LSS — Life-skills support

MDE — Multidisciplinary evaluation

MDT — Multidisciplinary team

MG — Mentally gifted

MH — Multihandicapped

MR — Mental retardation

OT - Occupational therapist

PDD — Pervasive developmental disability

PL 94-142 — Education for All Handicapped Children Act

PT — Physical therapist

SB — Spina bifida

TAT — Teacher assistance teams

TMR — Trainable mentally retarded

VI — Visually impaired

K: KICKING OFF THE PROJECT

Because the thought of inclusion may be terrifying for regular education staff, schools must tread lightly in the beginning.

Schools need to have a well-developed plan which will encourage staff to kick off the complex change process, making schools a more rewarding atmosphere for all. District goals and mission statements should be in line and share a common long-term vision for students.

Many schools take at least one year to plan for the change. Some districts begin by selectively placing identified students in one "regular" class period a day. Other districts begin by returning students from residential centers to neighborhood schools the first year, simple mainstreaming for special classes and homeroom the second year, and providing in-class instruction the following year.

The initial step toward inclusion begins with staff development and awareness. Understanding of the teaming process familiarizes staff with collaboration and problem solving. Until this time most teachers have taught in classes with doors closed and in isolation. Assure staff that inclusion is not isolation, that "none of us is as smart as all of us." Time must be provided in the planning as well as in the implementation stage so the staff feels adequately prepared and ready for collaboration.

"The initial step toward inclusion begins with staff development and awareness."

Encourage all staff to see that inclusion works. Invite speakers and visit districts where inclusion is working. Encourage teachers to talk to students and parents who have been involved in inclusion.

The community and all parents must be informed of the change. Task forces may be formed to share in the process. Districts should allow for voluntary involvement of staff during the implementation stages. Recruiting positive staff ensures that success will breed success.

Tips for Kicking Off the Project

1. Develop mission, vision, or belief statements.

2. Share your visions from the bottom up. Ask "What do we want as final outcomes for students?" Our vision is to develop a community of enthusiastic, caring individuals which encourages optimal growth while celebrating individual differences.

3. Assess skills of participants, assist in developing skills.

4. Provide needed incentives, goals, and rewards to ensure success for all.

5. Have resources available on staff, in libraries, bring in consultants as needed. Develop a parent resource center in the school library.

6. Develop a working action plan, understandable to all.

7. Include administrators, school personnel, and community on a task force.

8. Allow for voluntary participation of staff during phase-in period.

9. Identify special student population and match to the correct placement in regular classes.

10. Encourage special educators to lead staff workshops.

11. Provide workshops in: collaboration, cooperative learning, whole language, teaming, assessment, lesson adaptations, and multiage grouping.

12. Develop workable schedules for support staff.

13. Allow for collaborative planning time in the daily schedule.

14. Prepare students for inclusion through assemblies, puppets shows, videos, peer and adult speakers.

Developing an Action Plan

Designate where your school's assistance will come from (consultants, special education supervisors, administration).

Discuss specifically where students and staff are in the inclusion process.

Determine how much further the staff needs to go in order to reach goals.

In detail, describe who will be vital to your school-wide commitment. Decide who will be doing what, when, and how.

Determine what skills will be needed by staff and how to obtain the necessary skills.

Prioritize actions needed to be successful.

Determine a scheduled meeting time to reflect upon accomplishments and adjust goals.

Make the best use of available support.

Continue to go forth.

Purpose:

To develop a step-by-step action plan for an elementary school to facilitate inclusion.

Procedure:

Begin by sharing and expressing your school's dream for students. Allow staff participants to correlate personal values with ideas and commitment.

16 Skills a Staff Needs for Successful Inclusion

Inclusion is not an event that happens overnight. In order to make a smooth transition from isolating to accepting special needs students, schools must begin slowly and provide staff with necessary skills to be comfortable in the process.

"Inclusion is not an event that happens overnight."

1. Cooperative learning techniques

2. School-based teaming process

3. Collaborative techniques

4. Authentic assessment strategies – portfolios, anecdotal record keeping

5. Understanding of the IEP process (What is it? How does it look? How to incorporate student's strengths? How to implement in regular classroom setting?)

6. How to make curricular adaptations – teach to individual strengths and meet diverse needs in regular classroom setting

7. Use of facilitated communication devices (keyboards and alphabet displays to foster nonverbal communication)

8. Involving parents as partners (IEP process, aides, advocates)

9. Peer coaching (staff and students)

10. Establishing peer and cross-age tutors

11. Making the best use of instructional assistants within the regular classroom setting

12. Dispelling the special education myth (share knowledge, eliminate jargon, define old labels)

13. Handling challenging behaviors

14. Developing support systems

15. How to use common planning time and scheduling tips to facilitate the process

16. Understanding the role of special educators and their instructional adaptations

Inclusion Education Journey

A school-based continuum to assist in planning for a successful inclusive program

Classroom Practices

	Always	Occasionally	Seldom	Not at this time
1. Student receives same type and frequency of classroom/school responsibilities as peers.	☐	☐	☐	☐
2. Student receives same type of feedback regarding performance as peers.	☐	☐	☐	☐
3. Student is aware of consistent classroom goals and instructional procedures.	☐	☐	☐	☐
4. Student and classmates are provided with a variety of means to communicate and opportunities to do so.	☐	☐	☐	☐
5. Student sits *with* classmates in natural classroom setting.	☐	☐	☐	☐
6. Adult aides/assistants facilitate student-peer interaction.	☐	☐	☐	☐
7. Instructional methods encourage student interaction and active participation in learning.	☐	☐	☐	☐
8. Support services are provided in typical environments and encourage class participation.	☐	☐	☐	☐
9. Student attends general education homeroom and has a typical daily schedule.	☐	☐	☐	☐
10. Student attends lunch and recess *with* classmates.	☐	☐	☐	☐
11. Student's classroom transitions are the same as classmates, providing extra time if necessary.	☐	☐	☐	☐

Inclusion Education Journey (continued)

School-Wide Practices

	Always	Occasionally	Seldom	Not at this time
1. Student attends neighborhood school with same age peers.	☐	☐	☐	☐
2. Student arrives and leaves school with age-appropriate peers using common transportation.	☐	☐	☐	☐
3. Student progresses through grade levels with peers.	☐	☐	☐	☐
4. "People first" language is used, rather than disability descriptors. (John is a first grader versus John is a learning support student.)	☐	☐	☐	☐
5. Student's supplies, clothing and personal accessories are typical and age-appropriate.	☐	☐	☐	☐
6. Student uses same lavatory and is provided with the same privacy as classmates.	☐	☐	☐	☐
7. Student's work is displayed in the identical manner as classmates.	☐	☐	☐	☐
8. Student particpates in typical school and extracurricular activities, being provided with same opportunities for involvement.	☐	☐	☐	☐
9. Student is included in typical homeroom student counts, bulletin boards, and school-wide programs.	☐	☐	☐	☐
10. Student has same opportunity/choice of electives as classmates with adaptations occurring as needed.	☐	☐	☐	☐
11. Natural proportions are maintained in the school and in the classroom, and student diversity reflects the community at large.	☐	☐	☐	☐

Teachers' Publishing Group

Inclusion Education Journey (continued)

Team Practices

	Always	Occasionally	Seldom	Not at this time
1. The core team includes family, staff involved with the child and all members participating equally.	☐	☐	☐	☐
2. All team members are welcomed and valued equally.	☐	☐	☐	☐
3. Staff provide support/collaboration at meetings as needed.	☐	☐	☐	☐
4. Support staff/special education staff provide on-site training of instructional procedures as needed.	☐	☐	☐	☐
5. General education specialists participate as needed in the team planning process.	☐	☐	☐	☐
6. Team members understand and adhere to classroom parameters as described by classroom teachers.	☐	☐	☐	☐
7. Evaluation responsibilities are specifically identified and assigned to team members.	☐	☐	☐	☐
8. Team members provide ongoing support to the classroom teacher.	☐	☐	☐	☐
9. The team communicates regularly and efficiently, checking with regular education teacher regarding success on interventions.	☐	☐	☐	☐
10. Meetings occur on a regular and reasonable basis, with members being given adequate notification.	☐	☐	☐	☐
11. Meetings are punctual and efficient.	☐	☐	☐	☐

Team Practices Continued

	Always	Occasionally	Seldom	Not at this time
12. Meetings are conducted at times team members can participate, times are established from the beginning of year (e.g., every Monday, Wednesday from 7:30-8:30).	☐	☐	☐	☐
13. Meetings have set, mutually agreed-upon agendas. Agendas are previewed before meetings.	☐	☐	☐	☐
14. There are regular, clear procedures for record keeping and follow up. Notes are shared after meetings.	☐	☐	☐	☐
15. Necessary team roles are assigned and rotate. Members are active participants.	☐	☐	☐	☐

L: LESSON ADAPTATIONS

Rather than question what to teach when including all children in the regular classroom, it is more crucial for teachers to vary how they teach in order to accommodate differently-abled children.

Instead of paper/pencil activities teachers can use small group instruction, cooperative learning, group problem solving, a variety of assessment methods, learning centers, and projects to involve students actively in learning.

In order to support children in a typical classroom setting, regular and special educators need time to collaborate and develop the adaptations needed for success by individual students.

Lesson adaptations should match the individual level and rate of learning. Differently-abled children may require longer time periods to complete tasks and need more frequent repetitions in instructions.

Teachers must feel comfortable changing the response mode for students. Those who are creative in lesson planning and adaptations assist their students in developing feelings of self-worth and self-satisfaction while enabling them to take risks in the learning environment.

Tips for Lesson Adaptations

1. Limit the length of time required for high-level activities.

2. Allow students to assume various classroom roles (distributing paper, activating AV equipment, setting up snacks), while some work on detailed reports.

3. Provide active learning centers such as a class store, baking projects, and bake sales so students can see their work earn money.

4. Provide multilevel learning objectives.

5. Keep all goals and objectives age-appropriate.

6. Organize learning centers for various needs and learning styles.

7. Accept that all children do not need to meet the same educational goals at the same time.

Sample Accommodations

Instead of asking children to raise their hands to answer questions, have them point to their nose if someone says a true statement, or have them flip yes and no cards in response. Shorten assignments and match instructional level to ability as in the following examples:

Whole Language:

Instead of reading *Charlotte's Web*, children may listen to a condensed taped version and make a yarn web.

Some children may write independent thank you notes to the nurse on Nurse's Day, others may copy a class note. An included child may point to pictures showing what a nurse does.

Family Living:

While most students draw pictures of their families, label roles of each member, or make a family tree, one individual may be pointing to individual Polaroid snapshots of his or her family as named by his teaching assistant.

Science:

A typical goal for primary children is to "identify temperature." Some children will be required to identify, use, read, and compare Celsius and Fahrenheit thermometers. Others may distinguish molecular movements at different temperatures. A differently-abled child may be given cups filled with soda, coffee, soup, or milk and have to match "hot" or "cold" labels.

Math:

When learning about money, some children add and regroup dollars and cents. A second group labels or sorts nickels, dimes, and pennies by appearance. A third group picks pennies out of a given pile of coins.

Theme Study:

During a thematic unit on owls, some students may be engaged in a creative writing project while others may be tracing the word "owl" in jello.

In-Class Adaptions

Goal	Objectives/Activities	Materials/Adaptations
Subject: Music		
Participate in group singing.	**Timmy:** Will sing and do motions "in a cottage" with the group.	Pictures Tapes Tape recorder
	Patty: Will stay in the group for the duration of the song.	
	Sue: Will activate tape recorder.	
Subject: Reading		
Read and comprehend *It's Halloween, Dear Dragon*.	**Timmy:** Will read story and place five sentence strips from the story in order.	Book Sentence strips Word cards Pointer as needed
	Patty: Will point to pictures in the book and match to one-word descriptions.	
	Sue: Will point to pictures as descriptions are read.	
Subject: Math		
Increase accuracy of computational skills.	**Timmy:** Will complete five addition problems with regrouping.	Worksheet Calculator Salt box
	Patty: Will use a calculator to complete five word problems.	
	Sue: Will trace numerals 1-5 in salt box.	

Aimee's Day

	Classroom Activties	Aimee's Activities
8:45	Enter school Locate room	Enter school Locate room
8:55	Bathroom/drinks	Bathroom – more time is needed for an aide to assist.
9:00	Announcements	
9:10	Diary Time	Diary – Aimee keeps a pictorial diary. Magazines are located and peers assist in cutting. Any spoken words are written down.
9:30	Sharing/Rug Time	Sharing/Rug Time Aimee is encouraged to hold up her pictures as peers read words.
10:00	Book Sharing – Teacher and volunteers listen to children read trade books	Aimee will get materials organized, check daily schedule, feed class pet.
10:15		Aimee will prepare snack for self, then join peers.
10:30	Continue reading	Aimee will go to library with a cross-age tutor. They choose a book, tutor reads, she points to pictures.
11:00	Lunch/Recess	Lunch/Recess – Aimee sits with friends. Volunteer aide is close.
12:00	Story	Aimee will sit with peers to listen. Tapes are available if needed.
12:15	Bathroom	Aimee is with aide in restroom.
12:30	Math – The class is involved with regrouping in addition Learning Centers to match individual needs.	Math – Aimee is working with math manipulatives matching numerals 1-5 with sets. Peer assistance as needed.
1:30	Recess	Recess
2:00	Specials	Aimee is fully included in these classes.
3:00	Social studies, health or science	Aimee joins classmates by listening and observing. There may be nonverbal communication. Aimee is involved with cooperative learning projects.
3:30	Dismissal	Dismissal – Aimee is assisted with dismissal, leaves with peers.

Teachers' Publishing Group

M: MAPS

In planning the day-to-day events for included children, many schools have implemented the McGill Action Planning System (MAPS). This program was developed by Evelyn Lusthaus and Marsha Forest (1987) and assists adults with visualizing the whole child and his or her needs. (See *Educating All Students in the Mainstream of Regular Education*, edited by Susan Stainback, William Stainback, and Marsha Forest, published by Paul H. Brookes for a full description of MAPS.)

The essence of this plan is to assist schools with the integration process and development of in-class success. The key players in the planning process should include the student, the student's peers, parents or caregivers, and any staff involved with the student (classroom teachers, special education teachers, assistants, and support staff).

The ultimate goal of MAPS is to provide any student with the opportunity to be successfully integrated while enhancing friendships. Vital to this process is the fact that the school is taking time to validate parental concerns and emotions.

Typically, many parents are more at ease during a MAPS planning session if they are given the questions prior to the meeting. This allows parents to prepare and bring necessary documentation with them.

If staff members attending the MAPS meeting have never been part of the process, it is advantageous to also prepare them for the

"The ultimate goal of MAPS is to provide any student with the opportunity to be successfully integrated while enhancing friendships."

type of questions asked, possible replies, and how the meeting will be run. The process works smoothly if one team member (principal, guidance counselor, or classroom teacher), who has established a comfortable rapport with the family, facilitates the process/meeting. Another team member needs to be responsible for being the recorder and distributing gathered information at a later date.

This information will be used to develop an action plan for the included child.

By incorporating peers and siblings into the process, the adult-centered perspective becomes more child-centered. Planning emphasizes a child's gifts, talents, and abilities rather than "disabilities."

Although developed primarily for inclusion, this kind of sharing works well for all children. Many classroom teachers adapt this process for all parent conferences.

The MAPS Process

The MAPS process may look like this:

Facilitator to parent/caregiver:

1. Tell us about_____'s history – pregnancy, birth, development, school thus far. (Parents appreciate having someone who will listen to their story and empathize with them.)

2. What are your hopes and dreams for_____and _____'s future? (All members of the MAPS meeting should be encouraged to share their visions. The diversity of the planning team will provide a wide range of responses. Often parental responses revolve around social acceptance and lifelong independence while educators' responses tend to revolve around learning issues. Particular attention needs to be given to the student's and the peer's responses if they are present.)

3. What fears or nightmares do you have regarding_____? (Typically a parent may fear social rejection, lack of friends, or eventual institutionalization. Student fears often parallel those of the caregiver. Staff nightmares tend to be educational fears – not meeting IEP goals, inability to collaborate to meet needs, not enough time, etc.)

4. Tell me, who is_____? (In a brainstorming round-robin fashion, all participants at the meeting take a turn giving a one-word description of the student.)

5. In your opinion, what do you think_____likes? (Again, in a round-robin style each person contributes what s/he thinks the child enjoys in life.)

6. Speaking positively, what do you see as _____'s gifts, talents, strengths? (This emphasizes the positive aspects of the child's life rather than focusing on deficits.)

7. What do you see as_____'s needs, whether they be social, emotional, physical, or intellectual?

8. How can we provide an ideal day for _____ here at school?

9. As a parent, describe your child in five adjectives.

At the conclusion of the MAPS meeting a skeletal plan for the child will start to form. The team is encouraged to analyze a typical class schedule and reflect upon whether the child should do the required activities and if accommodations are necessary to ensure success. (For an example of how the form could be filled out, see page 176 .)

MAPS Meeting Plan

An Adapted MAPS Meeting Plan may look like this:

STUDENT NAME:_____

DATE OF MEETING:_____

THOSE IN ATTENDANCE:_____

_____

_____

FACILITATOR:_____

RECORDER:_____

1. Tell us about _____'s history.

2. What are your hopes and dreams for _____'s future?

3. Describe your fears or nightmares regarding_____.

4. Tell me, who is_____?

5. In your opinion, what do you think_____likes.

6. Speaking positively, what do you see as_____'s strengths, gifts, talents?

7. What physical, social, emotional, or academic needs does _____ have?

8. Working as an educational team, how can we provide an ideal day for

_____ here at school?

9. As a parent describe your child in five words.

N: NEIGHBORHOODS

Past practice has been that children with severe disabilities often had their educational needs met at segregated sites, often far from their neighborhood school.

Through inclusion, public schools are beginning to welcome back into the fold those children whose needs had been met elsewhere. Students return to their neighborhood schools and are placed in age-appropriate, typical classrooms where they would have been assigned if not for a label. Class size should be taken into consideration when placing children and assignments should match a child's needs to a teacher's ability to meet those needs.

Dumping large numbers of special needs students in a single classroom is not in the best interest of children or teacher. Such a practice would encourage labeling to continue. Peers would see the situation as "Mrs. Smith's class with the special education pod," for example. Through evenly distributing special needs children through-out their age-appropriate grades, there will be ample opportunity for role modeling and appropriate social and academic interactions.

Children should be educated with the peers they see daily around their home. These are the first children they naturally bond with. These are the friends they may keep throughout their school life.

"Children should be educated with the peers they see daily around their home."

Tips for Addressing Neighborhoods

1. Children are not indiscriminately dumped into regular education settings without the support of special education personnel.

2. Teachers who have been adequately prepared for inclusion are called upon first.

3. Success is contagious. Staff members who are comfortable with differently-abled children will eagerly discuss their success stories and help put others at ease.

4. Use "the principle of natural proportions" when assigning children to neighborhood schools and classroom settings. Place children proportionately in regular rooms without overloading some teachers.

5. Modify neighborhood transportation as needed. Check to see that buses can transport all children together to and from school. If specialized buses are needed, often typical children will volunteer to ride on those modified buses with others.

A Letter from Kelsey

As classroom teachers we often forget about the effect siblings have on our students. A third-grade student who wanted her brother to attend their neighborhood school wrote the following letter to her principal. These eloquently expressed sentiments reflect the true meaning of inclusion.

Dear Mrs. O'Connor,

I know you are a very busy principal, but I wanted to talk to you about my very special brother. His name is Timmy. Timmy always makes me happy, even when I feel very sad. He waits for me at our front door every day when I get home from school. He laughs when I walk in. I read him a story each night at bedtime. He really loves to hear The Little Monster story books. Timmy never forgets to give me a hug and a slobbery kiss when I finish. He is a great brother even though he is only five.

Some days I feel sad when I think about Timmy. You see, everyone says he's mentally retarded. My mom says he has Down Syndrome. Sometimes she cries when she whispers those words. But I am proud of Timmy.

Timmy goes to a special school that is far away from my school. He gets picked up each day in a special van. There are lots of kids on the van like Timmy. Some are even more handicapped, my mom says.

I feel sad that Timmy can't go on my bus to school. I don't understand it. He would be good in kindergarten. He likes stories. I even showed him how to fingerpaint. My mom says the teachers aren't ready for Timmy. I tell her we have nice teachers at our school who act like they like all the kids.

Timmy doesn't know how it feels to ride on my bus and walk from the bus stop back to our house all alone. But I could help him, and so would the big kids on the bus.

Timmy never got invited to a birthday party. His friends at his school are from all over the city. I know he'd love to blow a party horn.

He never sees our school plays and assemblies. Timmy never got to eat in a cafeteria with friends. I don't even think he knows about the best part of school — recess!

I tell Mom that he could learn if somebody would talk slowly enough and make his work look like play. My mom always says, "someday."

Won't you please help my little brother have his "someday" today? You could love Timmy just like I do.

Your friend,
Kelsey Dorman
Grade 3

> **"Won't you please help my little brother have his 'someday' today?"**

O: ORGANIZING

Once a school has adopted an inclusion policy, the first question many educators ask is "How do I organize the physical make-up of my classroom to meet such diverse needs?"

First, teachers need to be aware of the diversities they need to accommodate. The physical layout of the room should allow for flexibility in accommodating various types of furniture.

Teachers who are aware of the range of needs in their classrooms and have the necessary preparation time to organize have classrooms that are a more welcome home to all children.

"The physical layout of the room should allow for flexibility in accommodating various types of furniture."

Tips on Organizing

1. Develop a needs assessment inventory for included children (see page 93).

2. Measure assistive devices, wheelchairs, walkers before school begins to ensure adequate movement and space within the room and through doors. Measure tables and desks to be certain wheelchairs can fit under them.

3. Sensitize support staff and children to the usage of any assistive devices. Allow other children to "try out" this equipment.

4. Encourage students to share table supplies that are kept in a tote rather than individual supplies. This develops a feeling of "our" crayons rather than "my" crayons.

5. Place labels on cupboards, closets, and storage cabinets to make it easier for children and staff to get supplies.

6. Place children with visual or hearing impairments close to instruction.

7. Keep easily distracted children away from heaters or blowers.

8. Separate active learning centers from quiet work space. Keep specific instructions on the backs of centers and folders so assistants or tutors do not have to interrupt your lessons for directions and goals of the learning centers.

9. Provide an isolated "office" area in the room. This desk with a study carrel can be a chosen spot for children who sense when they are over-stimulated.

10. Chairs must be pushed under tables or desks to lessen chances of someone falling.

11. Encourage children to take an active role in the room arrangement. Keep furniture in a consistent location. If classrooms are rearranged, children who are visually impaired must rehearse getting around the room.

12. One child-sized rocker should be placed in each room. Some children find comfort in taking time out from academics to rock their cares away.

13. Provide a quiet reading or lounge area for children. A clawfoot bathtub filled with quilts and pillows makes a unique reading area.

14. Remove the teacher's desk if possible. Teachers who are not the focus of the classroom often do not need a desk.

15. Provide adequate space for support personnel and their supplies. Use portable shelves and stacking cartons if extra space is needed.

16. Allow for storage of language masters (auditory/visual reinforcement); tape recorders (for stories, group review, relaxation music, and process writing dictation); talking calculators (for visually impaired math review); and for facilitated communication and other assistive devices.

17. Provide open space areas for in-class physical and occupational therapy.

18. Use group tables instead of individual desks. If only desks are available, push them into groups or neighborhoods.

"Teachers who are not the focus of the classroom often do not need a desk."

Chair Packs and Pockets

Chair packs slip over backs of chairs to hold papers and projects to go home. This eliminates the necessity of children always moving to cubbies or mailboxes to deposit papers. Chair packs can easily be made by sewing a strip of material across the bottom of a pillowcase and slipping the open edge of the pillowcase over the child's chair. Or, a old pair of jeans can be shortened at the knees, sewn shut where shortened and slipped over a chair to provide a backpack for the chair.

Directions for Making Chair Pockets:

1. Each pocket uses a 36" x 30" piece of sturdy fabric.

2. On each piece of fabric, turn down one of the 30" ends 3/8" and then once again to cover the raw edge. Stitch.

3. Fold fabric in half lengthwise with right sides together. Sew a seam along the 36" side and then down the 30" side (not the folded end). Leave the top open.

4. Turn inside out. Iron the edges flat. Top stitch 1/8" along the closed short end.

5. Fold the closed end (short end) up 12" and sew 1/8" along the three sides of the pocket, leaving the fourth side open to form pocket opening.

6. Attach velcro strips (I use 2 1/2") to hold it in place on the child's chair.

7. Dimensions may need to be adjusted according to chair size. This works with chairs used for 5-to 7-year-olds.

8. Hint: before beginning on good material always try first on scrap fabric.

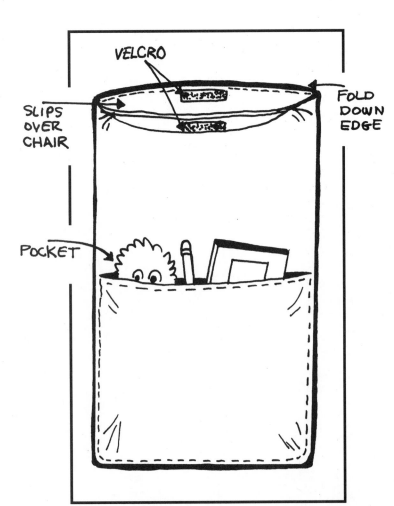

VELCRO

SLIPS OVER CHAIR

FOLD DOWN EDGE

POCKET

Student Needs Assessment

It is helpful to have the special education staff complete this form before the child is placed in the regular education classroom.

NAME:_____

HOMEBASE TEACHER:_____

SPECIAL EDUCATION STAFF:_____

SUPPORT STAFF:_____

1. List any supportive or assistive devices used with this child (wheelchair, walker, special computers, large print books, behavior management program, etc.).

2. List any adapted furniture needed (special desks, seat cushions, rocking chairs, changing tables).

3. List the names of resource personnel who will sensitize or help students and staff understand the use of special classroom equipment.

4. List the telephone number of those responsible for repairing such devices.

5. Are any other classroom adaptations needed?

Inclusive Needs Assessment

Program Practices

The practices identified below are distinctive of reputable, inclusive programs for students with severe disabilities. Consider the extent to which these practices are reflected in your school.

Curricular Planning	Current practice	In discussion stage	Not considered at this time
1. Student IEPs are activity-referenced, addressing functional skills taught in a variety of settings.	☐	☐	☐
2. Individualized adaptations are used, when necessary, to increase student participation and independence.	☐	☐	☐
3. An educative approach to the management of challenging behavior is utilized.	☐	☐	☐
4. Educational programs for students with severe disabilities reflect a "futures" orientation (preparing for tomorrow's challenge).	☐	☐	☐
5. Planned and comprehensive efforts are made to facilitate the development of social relationships between students with disabilities and their typical age-appropriate peers.	☐	☐	☐

Classroom Settings and Procedures

1. Student-specific schedules are developed by matching student needs and activities in the school and community.	☐	☐	☐
2. Students have the opportunity to learn in a variety of instructional arrangements, including pairs, small group, and large group arrangements.	☐	☐	☐
3. Individualized adaptations are used, when necessary, to increase student participation and independence.	☐	☐	☐

Classroom Settings and Procedures

	Current practice	In discussion stage	Not considered at this time
4. Curricular adaptations are planned and used to accommodate diverse student needs in the typical classroom setting.	☐	☐	☐
5. The classroom settings in which the student is placed are chronologically age-appropriate.	☐	☐	☐
6. Normalized evaluation procedures are utilized to assess progress relative to IEP goals and guide instructional decision making for individual learners.	☐	☐	☐

Interactions with Typical Peers

	Current practice	In discussion stage	Not considered at this time
1. Students with diverse needs have multiple and varied opportunities for involvement with typical peers.	☐	☐	☐
2. Involvement with typical peers occurs in both teaching and nonteaching relationships.	☐	☐	☐
3. Opportunities for integration are reflected in student IEP goals.	☐	☐	☐
4. Students are provided with opportunities for after-school social interactions.	☐	☐	☐

Home-School Collaboration

	Current practice	In discussion stage	Not considered at this time
1. A system of home-school communication that is mutually agreed upon by parents and staff is employed.	☐	☐	☐
2. A process is utilized to ensure that parent priorities are incorporated into a student's IEP and educational program.	☐	☐	☐
3. Parents receive frequent feedback about their child's school progress.	☐	☐	☐
4. Parents are encouraged to participate in parent groups at the school.	☐	☐	☐
5. Parents of students with severe disabilities are informed of all school activities.	☐	☐	☐

Inclusive Needs Assessment

Staff Integration

Collaboration with other faculty and staff members occurs within an expanding range of activities as all students become integral members of the school population.

	Current practice	In discussion stage	Not considered at this time
1. Special education staff assumes school-wide responsibilities (supervisory duties, extracurricular activities) in the same manner as their general education colleagues	☐	☐	☐
2. Special education staff participate in faculty meetings and other school-related committees.	☐	☐	☐
3. Related service staff use an integrated approach to the delivery of therapy.	☐	☐	☐
4. Special educators serve as instructional resources to general educators in approaches to accommodate diversity in the classroom.	☐	☐	☐
5. Co-teaching between special and general educators is encouraged as a means of meeting the individual needs of students in the classroom.	☐	☐	☐
6. Adequate time is provided for staff collaboration.	☐	☐	☐
7. Special educators as well as regular educators are members of a school-based team.	☐	☐	☐

Teachers' Publishing Group

Enhancing Self Esteem

Faculty and students model the behavior of special educators as they form instructional and social relationships with special needs students.

	Current practice	In discussion stage	Not considered at this time
1. If a special education classroom is in the school, it is located in proximity to age-appropriate regular education classes.	☐	☐	☐
2. Environment in special education classrooms, (if present) are age-appropriate.	☐	☐	☐
3. Language that emphasizes the person rather than the disability is used in written materials and conversation.	☐	☐	☐
4. Staff behavior reflects respect and a belief in the competence of all students.	☐	☐	☐
5. Discussions about students do not occur in their presence as if they were not there.	☐	☐	☐
6. Materials used with students with disabilities are age-appropriate.	☐	☐	☐
7. Activities in which students with disabilities are involved are age-appropriate.	☐	☐	☐

Inclusive Needs Assessment

Staff Preparation

Inclusion places new expectations on staff members involved in the delivery of instruction to students with severe disabilities. Consider the extent to which instructional staff feel prepared for their role in this program.

	Current practice	In discussion stage	Not considered at this time
1. Opportunities are available to visit existing programs to observe and learn about quality practices for the education of students with severe disabilities in regular schools and classes.	☐	☐	☐

2. Staff have the necessary training in these program practices:

	Current practice	In discussion stage	Not considered at this time
• Rationale/philosophy of integrated and inclusive programs	☐	☐	☐
• Integration/inclusion strategies	☐	☐	☐
• Functional curriculum	☐	☐	☐
• Curricular adaptation strategies	☐	☐	☐
• Alternative performance strategies	☐	☐	☐
• Collaboration and teamwork skills	☐	☐	☐
• Positive approaches to behavior modification	☐	☐	☐
• Activity-based IEP development	☐	☐	☐
• Home-school collaboration strategies	☐	☐	☐
• Community-based instruction	☐	☐	☐
• Community-based vocational training	☐	☐	☐

Staff Preparation Continued

	Current practice	In discussion stage	Not considered at this time
• Transition	☐	☐	☐
• Ability awareness	☐	☐	☐
• Integrated delivery of related services	☐	☐	☐
• Awareness of descriptors such as CP, Down Syndrome, autism	☐	☐	☐

Teachers' Publishing Group

P: PARENTS

Parent involvement is a key to any successful educational program. Parents play an integral role in inclusion. In many cases, they have been a lone advocate of inclusion for their child. Their dream comes true when their child is integrated into a public school.

From the beginning, parents should be included in the school-based team, attend IEP meetings, and be active partners in the inclusion process. Parents have unique perceptions of their child's talents, strengths, weaknesses, and needs. As educators we need to tap into this valuable resource and encourage parental input as we design educational programs and plan future placements.

Parents who are involved in schools and support the educational programs will be the most effective advocates for a quality education for all children.

> *"Parents have unique perceptions of their child's talents, strengths, weaknesses, and needs."*

Tips Regarding Parents

1. Parents can help orient their child to his or her new classroom.

2. Ask parents to share videotapes of their special child or family albums with teachers and students.

3. Involve parents in child-centered discussions, sharing concerns with class members and children and staff throughout the building.

4. Hold informational meetings for the school's entire parental population before inclusion begins. Allow parents of both labeled and nonlabeled students to share questions and concerns.

5. Invite parents of special needs students to address PTO meetings. Both parents and children can address such meetings. Parents tend to respect and believe information shared by other parents.

6. Send newsletters home on a regular basis to continue the school partnership and keep parents informed of upcoming events or recent classroom milestones.

7. Ask parent volunteers to help in the school. They can help classroom teachers with projects, instruction, field trips, and classroom organization. They can help in school libraries, in whole language publishing centers, and with book sharing activities. Even parents with full-time jobs will often volunteer to do projects at home for teachers. They can prepare art materials, assemble learning stations, type students' stories, or organize materials.

8. Establish a parent lending library in your school's resource center.

Sample Parent Letter

Dear Parents,

We are very excited about this school year! There are so many things your child will learn – academic as well as life skills.

You may hear your child talk about a variety of teachers (list names of all support staff coming into the room). Your child will continue to spend a majority of his academic year with me, so please contact me with any concerns or questions.

By the use of team teaching, your child will be offered small group as well as individual support. This allows us to eliminate the former pull-out programs.

If you missed our informational meeting in the spring, please plan to attend our sharing meeting next week. We would also like to encourage you to sign up for a few of the volunteer activities listed below. We look forward to working with you.

Sincerely,

I am able to help with:

☐ Book sharing

☐ Recess aide

☐ Clerical assistant in class

☐ With projects at home

☐ As an in-class aide

☐ With field trips

☐ Learning center aide

☐ Other

The best time for me to volunteer is:

Monday	☐ a.m.	☐ p.m.
Tuesday	☐ a.m.	☐ p.m.
Wednesday	☐ a.m.	☐ p.m.
Thursday	☐ a.m.	☐ p.m.
Friday	☐ a.m..	☐ p.m.

Name_____Phone_____

Letter from Pat Jones

Parents like Pat Jones know firsthand the costs and rewards of inclusion. The following letter is reprinted with permission of the Missouri Parents Act (MPACT). The letter first appeared in the *Parent to Parent Newsletter*.

"...I have come to know, firsthand, that inclusion is very expensive indeed."

"For the past several years, I have argued on many occasions that, if inclusion of children with disabilities into regular education settings was done with careful planning and creativity, it would be no more costly than segregated and separate special education models. I have always tried to admit when I am mistaken. There has been a dramatic change in my perspective this year and I have come to know, firsthand, that inclusion is very expensive indeed.

Since our son has been included in his neighborhood high school, we have had to buy tickets to football games, tickets to basketball games, school yearbooks, tickets to the school mixers, and the battle of the bands. We have had requests from him for the "in" clothing and the "in" haircut and twice as many wallet photos for his school pictures to trade with friends. We have had to financially assist with dinner dates, corsages, and homecoming dance tickets, an event that created a need for a new sport coat, khakis, shirt, tie, boxers (!), and socks. And now, before we've even paid for that, comes the news he will need a letterman's jacket for his football manager's letter. And we're not even through the first quarter!

For those of you who know how challenging our son's behavior could be both at home and school, we are thrilled to share an additional cost associated with his inclusion. We pay big bucks for "Outstanding" marks in Citizenship on report cards. When we made the deal, believe me, we did not anticipate ever having to pay up. This quarter, he presented us with an "O" in all six of his classes.

Don't let anyone kid you about the cost of inclusion. It's significant. It may even cost more when it's creative and well-planned. And it seems the longer you do it, the more it costs. Someone even contacted us to join the parents' club and the football boosters. We're easy marks, though . . . because it's the most fun we've ever had spending money.

P.S. I had hoped to enclose a picture of our son when he entered school the morning he wore his letterman's jacket for the first time. I took the camera, but he was quickly lost in a sea of purple and white. Only I could have picked out the one who looked six inches taller than the day before!"

Preamble to the IEP

The following inventory to be completed by parents helps identify community living expectations for included students. This can be used in conjunction with the IEP, which focuses more on identifying academic needs and expectations, and with MAPS, which takes the child's social needs into account. When used together, the parent inventory, IEP, and MAPS help develop a more holistic picture of each child and allow for more effective planning. (See pages 173-183 for an example of how these different forms might be filled out for a particular child.)

Elementary Inventory of Parent Preferences

Student Name: _____ Student Age: _____ Grade: _____

Parent's Name: _____ Phone: (home) _____ (work) _____

Preschool Attended: _____ Previous School Attended: _____

Your response to the following questions will help identify areas that should be included on your child's Individual Education Plan for this year. This information will be used as a *starting point* in the development of your child's Individual Education Plan.

Community Living Skills

Activity/Skill	Does student currently do this?		What kind of help is needed?	Would you like student to work on this?	
Walk in neighborhood	Y	N	_____	Y	N
Obey traffic signs	Y	N	_____	Y	N
Eat at fast food restaurant	Y	N	_____	Y	N
Eat at sit down restaurant	Y	N	_____	Y	N
Eat in cafeteria	Y	N	_____	Y	N
Use vending machines	Y	N	_____	Y	N
Can locate house	Y	N	_____	Y	N
Say address	Y	N	_____	Y	N
Say phone number	Y	N	_____	Y	N
Recognize community helpers	Y	N	_____	Y	N
Can locate school	Y	N	_____	Y	N
Can locate classroom	Y	N	_____	Y	N
Can locate school bus/bus number	Y	N	_____	Y	N
Other _____	Y	N	_____	Y	N

Teachers' Publishing Group

Living Skills

Activity/Skill	Does student currently do this?		What kind of help is needed?	Would you like student to work on this?	
Food Preparation					
Use correct utensils	Y	N	_____	Y	N
Prepare simple snacks	Y	N	_____	Y	N
Pack lunch with assistance	Y	N	_____	Y	N
Eat unassisted	Y	N	_____	Y	N
Clothing Care					
Separate clothes	Y	N	_____	Y	N
Fold clothes	Y	N	_____	Y	N
Choose daily outfits	Y	N	_____	Y	N
Identify types of clothes	Y	N	_____	Y	N
Cleaning					
Could hand wash dishes	Y	N	_____	Y	N
Make bed	Y	N	_____	Y	N
Sweep floor	Y	N	_____	Y	N
Set/clear table at mealtime	Y	N	_____	Y	N
Take out garbage	Y	N	_____	Y	N
Dust furniture	Y	N	_____	Y	N
Straighten bedroom	Y	N	_____	Y	N
Pick up toys	Y	N	_____	Y	N

Living Skills

Activity/Skill	Does student currently do this?	What kind of help is needed?	Would you like student to work on this?
Other Domestic Skills			
Care for house plants	Y N	_____	Y N
Care for pet	Y N	_____	Y N
Help rake leaves	Y N	_____	Y N
Pick flowers/vegetables	Y N	_____	Y N
Other: _____	Y N	_____	Y N

Leisure Skills

Activity/Skill	Does student currently do this?	What kind of help is needed?	Would you like student to work on this?
Gross Motor Skills			
Skip	Y N	_____	Y N
Talk a walk	Y N	_____	Y N
Hop	Y N	_____	Y N
Play with frisbee	Y N	_____	Y N
Swim	Y N	_____	Y N
Play team sports	Y N	_____	Y N
Throw a ball	Y N	_____	Y N
Catch a ball	Y N	_____	Y N
Games/Crafts/Hobbies			
Read or look at books	Y N	_____	Y N
Play computer games	Y N	_____	Y N
Play video games	Y N	_____	Y N
Play card games	Y N	_____	Y N

Teachers' Publishing Group

Leisure Skills (Continued)

Activity/Skill	Does student currently do this?	What kind of help is needed?	Would you like student to work on this?
Games/Crafts/Hobbies (Continued)			
Play board games	Y N	_____	Y N
Can play alone	Y N	_____	Y N
Can share with others	Y N	_____	Y N
Listen to stories	Y N	_____	Y N
Choose favorite story	Y N	_____	Y N
Has favorite song/music	Y N	_____	Y N
Use paste	Y N	_____	Y N
Use scissors	Y N	_____	Y N
Do puzzles	Y N	_____	Y N
Can build with blocks	Y N	_____	Y N
Musical Activities			
Respond to music	Y N	_____	Y N
Use cassette	Y N	_____	Y N
Use radio	Y N	_____	Y N
Listen to music	Y N	_____	Y N
Attend Events/Places			
Go to mall/shopping	Y N	_____	Y N
Go to library	Y N	_____	Y N
Watch sporting event	Y N	_____	Y N
Go to a movie	Y N	_____	Y N

Leisure Skills (Continued)

Personal Skills

Activity/Skill	Does student currently do this?	What kind of help is needed?	Would you like student to work on this?
Other: _____	Y N		Y N
Communications Skills			
Answer telephone	Y N		Y N
Dial telephone	Y N		Y N
Talk with friends/family on phone	Y N		Y N
Relay personal information (name, phone number)	Y N		Y N
Seek information when needed	Y N		Y N
Seek help when needed	Y N		Y N
Self Care Skills			
Dress self	Y N		Y N
Button self	Y N		Y N
Zip self	Y N		Y N
Tie shoes	Y N		Y N
Select appropriate clothes	Y N		Y N
Locate restrooms	Y N		Y N
Wash hands and face	Y N		Y N

Personal Skills (Continued)

Activity/Skill	Does student currently do this?	What kind of help is needed?	Would you like student to work on this?
Brush teeth	Y N	_____	Y N
Bathe/shower alone	Y N	_____	Y N
Other: _____	Y N	_____	Y N
_____			

Work Skills

Work Habits			
Complete given chores	Y N	_____	Y N
Follow verbal directions	Y N	_____	Y N
Follow written directions	Y N	_____	Y N
Clean up toys/room	Y N	_____	Y N
Ask for assistance when needed	Y N	_____	Y N
Other: _____	Y N	_____	Y N
_____			

Looking into the Future

1. What accomplishments would you like your son or daughter to have after elementary school?

☐ Acceptance of self, others

☐ Appreciation for self-accomplishments

☐ Awareness of others' abilities and gifts

☐ Achievement on an individual academic basis

2. Describe how you will encourage the development of friendships with your son/daughter (in school and after school):

3. How would you like to be involved in the educational process at our elementary school?

Teachers' Publishing Group

Q: INCLUSION QUESTIONS

Ten Most Commonly Asked Questions Regarding Inclusion

1. Q. What is the real goal of inclusion?

A. Inclusion is providing an appropriate education program to all students in a regular class attended by nondisabled peers in a neighborhood school. The goal of inclusion is to allow a variety of children to learn and play side-by-side while ensuring success for all. Gone are the special education rooms which were formerly housed at the end of a hallway or in a broom closet. The former special education teachers are now working as part of a team in a regular classroom. Teachers are delivering instruction to children with a diverse range of learning needs. Staff members fully embrace the philosophy that each child belongs in a classroom that s/he would attend if not for a disability, for part, if not all of the school day.

> *"Teachers are delivering instruction to children with a diverse range of learning needs."*

2. Q. What can I do if there's not enough time to plan and collaborate with the special education teacher?

A. Make time! No matter how many minutes of planning time teachers are given during the day, there is always some new pressing matter for us to take care of. It can be implementing a new math program, discussing whole language, or working to become a multiage classroom. We are always busy and always taking more home to do each evening. Planning with your special education support person may mean taking a few minutes each Friday morning to discuss next week's lesson plan and how to incorporate Johnny into the lesson. It may mean asking your supervisor to allow for a common planning time per grade level with the special education aide freeing the special teacher to come to your planning meeting. It may mean you have to run ideas by each other in the parking lot or cafeteria line, but do it.

If we wait for someone to give us a gift of interrupted planning time we will be doing a disservice to the children. If the foundations for inclusion have been laid carefully, teachers will feel more at ease and have a greater understanding of instructional strategies that work. (See page 141 for creative, field-tested ideas for scheduling meeting time.)

3. Q. How can we change the attitude of staff members who resist any new change?

A. Those who say "I can't" need to get out of the way of those who are already doing it. The kiss of death to any new idea is forcing resisters to join before they are ready or able.

Teachers who believe that all children can have their needs met in their neighborhood schools with peers must lead the way for the resisters. We need to talk about the success in our classrooms, the way children learn from each other, the friendships that have developed, and the support that has been given to the process. Children can talk at faculty meetings and PTO meetings. Parents can discuss their apprehensions and the impact of inclusion. Resisters can be invited into our classrooms and to our meetings. We need to allow ample time to answer their questions and help dispel myths.

Unfortunately, not all teachers believe that all children can learn if we change the way material is delivered. These teachers cannot be forced to change. Placing certain children in their room could prove to be devastating to the program. If our success begins to breed success throughout the school, hesitant teachers will join us, but resisters will not.

4. Q. How will I schedule all of these supports coming in and out of my room?

"If our success begins to breed success throughout the school, hesitant teachers will join us, but resisters will not."

A. Scheduling support within the regular classroom will be no more difficult than trying to remember the old schedules of when to send children out of the room for services.

Classroom teachers need to sit down with the entire support staff before the school year begins to plan schedules according to the student's needs, IEP, and availability of special education staff. If a child needs support during the language arts portion of the day, the special education teacher or assistant should plan to be in the room for a portion of that time. Cooperative learning groups should be in place as well as peer tutoring or parent volunteers. If a child requires assistance in speech or language, that service should be scheduled during oral communication time in the day. When tentative schedules are in place for the beginning of the school year, the staff must be flexible enough to monitor and adjust them according to the needs of labeled and nonlabeled students and classroom teachers.

5. Q. What is the role of the special education teacher in the regular classroom?

A. Special education teachers will become coaches for regular education teachers and cheerleaders for their students' success. They will be responsible for interpreting the IEP, for assisting with classroom adaptations and instructional strategies, for collaborating with individual teachers and the team, for gathering materials, and for team teaching within the regular classroom. Special education teachers will become consultants for the regular classroom. They may be responsible for applying techniques from a special setting to the regular room, observing student progress, and making adjustments as needed. They may help adapt tests and train tutors.

Special education teachers will not come into the homebase setting and pull children to the back of the room every day to work one-to-one. They will become regular educators with a speciality in adaptive instruction and integration.

6. Q. How can one teacher teach to such a wide range of learning styles in the regular education classroom?

A. It is the teacher's job to meet the needs of all children assigned to his or her room. Even without inclusion, a teacher in a single-grade classroom may have students with at least a three-year span in ability. Public school

"Special education teachers will become coaches for regular education teachers and cheerleaders for their students' success."

students are guaranteed a free education which meets their learning needs.

When special needs children are placed in the classroom, a teacher should receive needed supports. That may not mean a full-time aide, but the teacher should be able to collaborate in and out of class with the special education teacher and have adult volunteers, cross-age and peer tutors available.

7. Q. How can teachers be assured that having labeled students in the classroom will not take time from normal or gifted students?

A. Students all benefit from having a variety of classmates together for role models and peer groups. By integrating a wide range of learners in a classroom, children develop an understanding of different learning styles, individual needs, and diversity.

Teachers must not have a classroom which only focuses on weaknesses of the population. If teachers are meeting the needs of only one student in their classroom or are giving only a few children their undivided attention, they are not being fair to other class members.

Often special needs children bring with them an array of materials and resources that other children can use. Many times support personnel will design lessons to include more than one child. Teaching assistants and volunteers should be instructed to meet the needs of all children in the classroom.

The mainstream of education is not a right to be earned by segregated children; it is a right that belongs to all children. It is our job as education professionals to combine our efforts and talents to meet all children's needs in our classrooms.

8. Q. How should differently-abled children be assessed within the regular education setting?

A. Assessment procedures used for all children need to be addressed. The old, traditional ABC method of grading needs to get in line with the process method of teaching. We allow students to express their feelings orally and in writing, teach them to edit and rewrite, encourage hands-on math and project-based science and social living, and allow them to read for enjoyment and gain necessary skills. Therefore, we need to eliminate assessments which are based on a lock-step method of grading and abstract responses.

Students need to be actively involved in planning for

"The mainstream of education is not a right to be earned by segregated children; it is a right that belongs to all children."

learning and evaluating their progress. Observation of classroom performance in desired activities needs to be noted. Children should be given a chance to apply what they have learned in real-life situations. Data needs to be gathered throughout the year to demonstrate individual growth and progress.

Classroom assessments must be ongoing throughout the year, with instruction matched to the child's learning style. Portfolios and anecdotal report cards demonstrate student growth and achievement. Report cards should document adaptations used for students, state the student's strengths, and be consistent with an individual's educational plan. Parents or caregivers should be given the opportunity to share in the report card and assessment procedure.

9. Q. What types of inservicing should be done to better prepare classroom teachers for inclusion?

A. Classroom teachers need a wide variety of skills and techniques to use even if there is no inclusion. Many of the gray-area children in the regular classroom require much teacher time and preparation because they often do not receive any supplemental services. Added to this are children who receive only assistance in speech or Chapter 1 and at no other time during the day.

All teachers can find comfort in learning to sharpen their "kid watching" skills. They become better observers and can identify strengths, weaknesses, and interests.

In addition, the following information and skills are valuable:

1. collaboration and team building skills;

2. familiarity with instructional adaptations needed by many children;

3. cooperative learning strategies;

4. understanding and implementing the whole language philosophy;

5. understanding IEPs and their implementation;

6. understanding special education terminology and jargon;

7. how to create child-centered classrooms;

8. planning for active learning and hands-on activities.

Teachers must become comfortable with individualizing education for all students. They must learn how to "shift gears" when teaching a whole group to meet individual needs.

"Classroom assessments must be ongoing throughout the year, with instruction matched to the child's learning style."

10. Q. How do we determine when inclusion is a mere juggling act and permit a time to pull out children out for special services?

A. Inclusion is a belief that services can be "pushed into" the regular education classroom instead of a child being pulled out. Each included student has an IEP in place that states what that child needs to learn. Teachers can help these students accomplish as many of their individual goals as possible in the classroom with their peers. Children need to be given the opportunity to develop appropriate social skills and peer relationships. They should feel like a member of the class instead of a visitor who comes and goes.

However, time spent in the classroom must be meaningful for all involved. There are cases when it is not appropriate or the "least restrictive environment," as required by law, for a child to be placed in a classroom for 100% of the instructional day.

When abstract learning activities are in place in the regular room, some children may benefit more from going into the community to learn about stores and post offices, etc., and develop necessary community living skills. It is better for students to participate in part of the classroom activities than to be excluded entirely.

When inservice programs and adequate support lessen classroom teachers' anxiety, more and more of them prefer that the included child receive as many of his or her needed supports as possible in the regular classroom.

"It is better for students to participate in part of the classroom activities than to be excluded entirely."

Inclusive Education Checklist

Before beginning an inclusion project, teachers should take a few moments to ask themselves some basic questions. The list on the following pages is not all encompassing but will assist in getting an inclusion project off the ground.

All across the the nation, classroom teachers and specialists are being asked to meet the daily challenge of educating all children within the "regular" classroom setting. In order to be truly inclusive, children need to be included in activities with age-appropriate peers in their home school setting. Neighborhood schools must now welcome back into the fold a variety of children who previously had been excluded or schooled at another site. The following checklist will provide an expedient avenue for the initial inclusive project.

School Community

	Implemented	Planning stage	Needs to be done
Is the school physically able to include all? (ramps, elevators, wheelchair access, lavatories, desks, etc.)	☐	☐	☐
Have *all* staff members received adequate inservice? (teachers, teacher assistants, nurses, custodians, secretaries, administrators, cafeteria workers, bus drivers)	☐	☐	☐
Is the school's mission statement in line with the inclusive philosophy of educating all children toward developing positive citizenship?	☐	☐	☐
Have support teams been initiated to ease staff, parents, and community into a "we" philosophy as opposed to an "I" philosophy?	☐	☐	☐
Is the staff able to collaborate on educational issues?	☐	☐	☐
Have the needs and IEPs of the included children been described in simple terms?	☐	☐	☐
Is the staff able to positively model the inclusive philosophy?	☐	☐	☐
Have parents and community task-force members been inserviced?	☐	☐	☐

School Community	Implemented	Planning stage	Needs to be done
Have the special education and regular education teachers been provided with adequate time to plan and implement?	☐	☐	☐
Have art, computer, library, music and physical education teachers become part of the teaming process?	☐	☐	☐
Is the school able to grasp the concept of all education is special and all teachers are special teachers?	☐	☐	☐
Have staff and student labels begun to disappear?	☐	☐	☐

Classroom Environment

	Implemented	Planning stage	Needs to be done
Have the children been prepared for the inclusive project?	☐	☐	☐
Has a variety of literature been used to enable the children to see and discuss acceptance of all?	☐	☐	☐
Have the children been exposed to speakers, videos, and movies which share disabilities?	☐	☐	☐
Is the classroom set up to facilitate movement for *all* children?	☐	☐	☐
Are there a variety of activities and centers available to meet a variety of learning styles?	☐	☐	☐
Is friendship an integral part of the school-wide curriculum?	☐	☐	☐
Are classroom rules and consequences written in a simple language, displayed for all to see, and frequently reviewed?	☐	☐	☐

Classroom Environment

	Implemented	Planning stage	Needs to be done
Are children and teachers able to communicate with each other or employ assistive devices as needed?	☐	☐	☐
Is the classroom philosophy one that encourages cooperative learning, peer partners, and cross-age study buddies?	☐	☐	☐
Are there positive peer role models for all children?	☐	☐	☐

Students' Rights

	Implemented	Planning stage	Needs to be done
Do all children enter the classroom at approximately the same time?	☐	☐	☐
Are the students situated in the classroom to facilitate their individual learning styles?	☐	☐	☐
Do all children engage in similar activities at the same time?	☐	☐	☐
Do all children, regardless of their label, receive the aid of a teacher assistant or specialist as needed within the regular classroom setting?	☐	☐	☐
Are all children made to feel welcome and seen as participating members of a classroom society?	☐	☐	☐
Are all children involved actively in classroom routines?	☐	☐	☐
Do all members of the classroom assist each other only when needed, while allowing for individual independence?	☐	☐	☐
Are all classmates taught at a developmentally appropriate level?	☐	☐	☐

Students' Rights

	Implemented	Planning stage	Needs to be done
Are all successes celebrated equally?	☐	☐	☐
Is adequate time provided for peer interactions? Are positive interactions encouraged?	☐	☐	☐
Are students able to accomplish individual goals in a regular classroom setting?	☐	☐	☐
Are all children set up to succeed in the regular classroom setting?	☐	☐	☐
Are parents and support staff available to rehearse with children their expected educational outcomes? (practice reading at home, listen to tapes, provide background experiences)	☐	☐	☐
Are all the children provided with immediate, positive feedback?	☐	☐	☐

R: RULES

Successful integration of students into their neighborhood school hinges upon an effective classroom management system. In any elementary classroom, rules set the tone for successes or failures of the whole group and must be designed to meet a variety of needs. Children who display any form of disruptive behavior rely on a consistent, well-managed classroom setting. Teachers need to be clear and direct when giving behavioral messages to children. Instead of "John, sit down and try to do this work, OK?" try "John, please sit down and stay in your seat until your math is finished."

Teachers should reinforce positive actions often, extinguish negative actions quickly, and check students individually to see if they understand and interpret rules correctly.

Classroom rules can govern and guide acceptable behaviors while instilling in children feelings of kindness, acceptance, and belonging.

Tips for Rules

"Praising positive behavior is more effective than responding to negative actions."

1. Maintain an orderly classroom.

2. Allow students to have a voice in decision making regarding rules.

3. Encourage one student per day to be your assistant in reviewing rules and consequences.

4. Develop student-centered rules.

5. As a joint effort, develop a "Classroom Bill of Rights" with contributions by all. Have all children sign it.

6. Ask children, "How do you want our room to look to visitors? Which rules enhance that feeling?"

7. Discuss the need for exceptions to rules. Brainstorm why you might have exceptions and how all children can forgive exceptions.

8. Catch children being good. Use a hole punch to punch a name tag on their desk each time they are behaving appropriately. Have a reward system in place – five punches earns extra computer time – 10 punches earns lunch with the principal.

9. Praising positive behavior is more effective than responding to negative actions.

10. Design instructional choices to reflect short-term behavioral goals. ("You may choose to do this activity sheet or develop a class collage for your project.")

11. Encourage parents to participate in enforcing rules. Send home a list of the classroom rules to be reviewed. Ask parents to sign the rules and call them at home or at work if major infractions occur.

12. Develop behavioral contracts if necessary.

13. Reward even the slightest improvements in a child's behavior.

14. Find any positive performance and praise! praise! praise!

Developing Rules with Your Class

Teachers can set a positive feeling tone in the classroom by developing clear, concise rules and consequences. These rules need to be designed by the entire class and allow for shared governance.

Teachers facilitate the process by discussing rules in society, who makes them, who breaks them, and what are the consequences of breaking rules.

Children are invited to brainstorm as a class why we have rules in school.

Children are given ownership in class rules by developing lists of acceptable/nonacceptable classroom behaviors.

Children work in groups of four to illustrate acceptable behaviors.

The following day the children are put in groups of four. Each group is given a plain placemat from a local restaurant. Children divide the placemat into four sections with a box in the center. They take two minutes to silently brainstorm (write quietly) as many classroom rules as they feel are important and write them in the four corners of the placemat. Next they share their rules and come to a consensus about one rule important to their group and write it in the center box. Gathered together on the rug once again, the children share their group's consensus and develop a list of important rules.

The class as a whole matches rules to appropriate consequences.

Younger children may need to do rebus rules and consequences.

Post classroom rules for all; review daily.

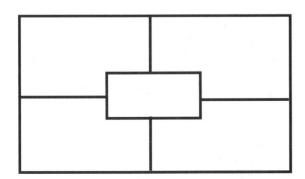

Placemat would look like this.

Sample Rules

I have the right to learn according to my needs. Nobody should make fun of me because of the way I learn.

I have the right to be my own person in this room. Nobody should laugh at me because of the way I look or act.

In our room we earn respect by doing our best. We show respect by treating others fairly.

We can solve our problems in Room 12 by talking not hurting.

Never hurt another person. Never destroy another person's work.

Teachers' Publishing Group

S: SUPPORT

Support in an inclusive classroom does not necessarily mean that a classroom teacher will receive a full-time teaching assistant or aide. Teachers can develop their own individual support network by visiting inclusive schools, observing in classrooms where inclusion is in place, becoming "kid watchers" regarding developmentally appropriate practices, and sharing fears, uncertainties, ideas, and strategies with other teachers.

Trust and collaboration among staff members are essential components in making inclusion work. Teachers need to be comfortable discussing problems and concerns. Classroom teachers should become proactive and invite special educators to answer their "what if" questions. The ultimate goal of the special educator is to become a coach for the classroom teacher and a cheerleader for the child's success. Special educators support the classroom teacher by: interpreting the IEP, defining IEP goals, developing specially designed instruc-

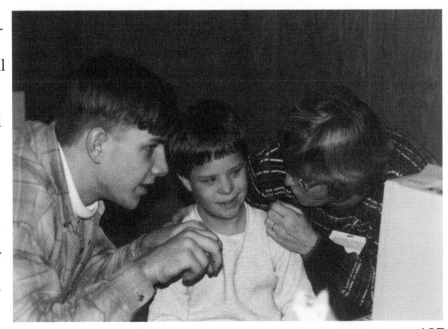

tion, assisting with instructional adaptations, and collaborating with planning of themes, lessons, and community-based instruction.

The following specialized support may also be provided students and teachers: occupational therapists enhance sensory motor/neurological techniques; physical therapists support children by helping them develop gross motor skills; speech/language clinicians assist with communication and language development; school psychologists interpret test results and observe children at work and play; and Chapter I teachers reinforce whole language skills and collaborate with classroom teachers in planning small group instruction.

"In inclusive classrooms, support is provided as a service, not a location."

In inclusive classrooms, support is provided as a service, not a location. In-class supports may take the look of volunteer aides, fifth graders helping in first or second grade, high school students who volunteer after school or during school to earn extra credit, senior citizen volunteers who are picked up at a retirement village on a school bus and brought to school to help, peer tutors, or cooperative learning groups.

Administrators who encourage new teaching strategies and instructional changes are also a valuable support for teachers and help them feel more comfortable taking risks and asking for help as needed.

If classroom teachers are lucky enough to receive a full-time aide, that person must be instructed as to how to best assist all children in the classroom. Aides should not hover over identified students and isolate them further from their peers. Many districts which have eliminated labels from children are also eliminating them from teachers. All teachers are hired to teach all children. The sign of an outstanding inclusive classroom is when a visitor enters that room and cannot identify labeled children or special education teachers.

Tips for Support

1. Familiarize support staff with commonly used prompts, cues, and rewards within the regular classroom.

2. Support staff should encourage socialization among children, not direct it.

3. Provide time for support staff to get together as a team and collaborate.

4. Provide adequate storage space for equipment needed by support personnel.

5. Display Polaroid pictures of support personnel with their job title and job description. This lessens the questions "Who is she?" "Why does he work in our room?"

6. Provide children with a desktop picture schedule of their helpers for the day.

7. Videotape each support person on the job to help children understand his or her role in the class.

Using Support Personnel in the Classroom

Purpose:

To demonstrate the integration of support personnel in a specific regular education project.

Procedure:

Third-grade students are assigned a research project on explorers.

Classroom Activities

Class brainstorms list of all explorers they know.

Individual children choose an explorer to research.

Children go to library to use card catalog.

Children begin reading and taking notes.

Children begin to take notes and write their paper.

Diane's Supported Activities

Diane sits in brainstorming circle, contributing if able. Peer partner available.

Diane and her high school volunteer choose a topic.

Special education teacher gathers books on table for Diane.

Diane chooses from books her special education teacher put on the library table.

Building team collaborates to suggest the following strategies for Diane: making a collage, making an illustrated timeline, role playing an interview with an explorer, illustrating another child's report, visiting the city museum. Additional support might be for an aide to read a chapter about the explorer, a high school aide to help with the timeline, an at-home parent volunteer to make costumes for the interview, or a classroom buddy to write the report for Diane to illustrate.

Teachers' Publishing Group

Checklist to Monitor Included Children's Progress

A simple monitoring checklist such as this enables teachers to be aware of classroom performances of children in different settings, particularly when a child may be working without the special education teacher in the classroom.

Student_____ Week of_____

	Homebase Teacher	Supporting Teacher
1. Cooperation with teacher	_____	_____
2. Classroom behavior	_____	_____
3. Completing classwork	_____	_____
4. Returning homework	_____	_____
5. Following directions	_____	_____
6. Classroom performance	_____	_____
7. Out-of-class behavior		

_____

_____

+ = Great job
* = Satisfactory
N = Needs improvement

Comments:_____

_____

Student Profile Sheet

Student Name_____Homebase Teacher_____
Special Education Teacher_____
Education Paraprofessional_____
Will the aide accompany the student?　　　Yes　　　No

Strengths	Weaknesses

Goals for	Suggested Activities for
Physical Education:	Physical Education:
Music:	Music:
Art:	Art:
Library:	Library:
Computer:	Computer:

Strategies for behaviorial intervention

Student interest

Medical concerns/Procedures to implement

A Principal's Observation Guide for the Inclusive, Natural Language Classroom

	Most of the Time				Seldom	
General Appearance **In this inclusive classroom:**						
Are the children placed in age-appropriate settings?	1	2	3	4	5	NA
Are the tables (or desks, only if necessary) arranged in small "neighborhood" settings rather than rows?	1	2	3	4	5	NA
Is adequate space provided to facilitate natural movement of all members?	1	2	3	4	5	NA
Are all children integrated naturally rather than some isolated in the back of the room?	1	2	3	4	5	NA
Are support personnel comfortable in the classroom?	1	2	3	4	5	NA
Is adequate space provided for adaptive or assistive teaching devices?	1	2	3	4	5	NA
Are support personnel moving freely in the room assisting any and all children?	1	2	3	4	5	NA
Are children encouraged to move freely from center to center?	1	2	3	4	5	NA
Is the noise level acceptable for social interaction and peer collaboration?	1	2	3	4	5	NA
Is there a wide variety of materials available for hands-on learning activities?	1	2	3	4	5	NA
Is there a quiet area provided for students' use?	1	2	3	4	5	NA
Are materials available at students' eye level?	1	2	3	4	5	NA

	Most of the Time				Seldom	
Is there an overall feeling of acceptance generated in the classroom?	1	2	3	4	5	NA

Curriculum

In this inclusive classroom:

Is experience the basis for learning?	1	2	3	4	5	NA
Do spoken and written language influence each other?	1	2	3	4	5	NA
Are children exposed to a wide variety of literature?	1	2	3	4	5	NA
Are children encouraged to understand that the purpose of reading is to construct meaning and enjoy the process?	1	2	3	4	5	NA
Is there time allotted daily for independent reading, writing, and activities?	1	2	3	4	5	NA
Does the teacher read aloud to all children more than once a day?	1	2	3	4	5	NA
Is there ample opportunity for journal writing, process writing, and story publication?	1	2	3	4	5	NA
Is time provided for individual reading/writing conferences?	1	2	3	4	5	NA
Is writing used as a natural response to literature?	1	2	3	4	5	NA
Does the teacher provide time for shared writing?	1	2	3	4	5	NA
Are all children provided listening experiences?	1	2	3	4	5	NA
Are children provided discussion time for self-evaluation and peer evaluation with writing?	1	2	3	4	5	NA

	Most of the Time				Seldom	
Does the teacher model correct language usage (spoken and written)?	1	2	3	4	5	NA
Are children encouraged to facilitate group discussions?	1	2	3	4	5	NA
Are logical thinking and problem solving fostered?	1	2	3	4	5	NA
Are numbers and numeration taught through concrete manipulation?	1	2	3	4	5	NA
Are opportunities provided to discover relationships among math skills and concepts?	1	2	3	4	5	NA
Is friendship a natural part of the curriculum?	1	2	3	4	5	NA

Teaching Strategies
In this inclusive classroom:

	Most of the Time				Seldom	
Is the teacher able to meet children's needs at their current developmental level?	1	2	3	4	5	NA
Is the teacher aware of individual learning channels?	1	2	3	4	5	NA
Is the material presented to meet all learning channels?	1	2	3	4	5	NA
Is adequate time provided for multisensory exploration?	1	2	3	4	5	NA
Does the teacher promote social interaction among learners?	1	2	3	4	5	NA
Are diverse strategies employed to promote discussion, higher level thinking skills, and multiple response techniques?	1	2	3	4	5	NA
Do cooperative learning groups actively involve all students?	1	2	3	4	5	NA

	Most of the Time				Seldom	
Are thematic units in place which integrate the curriculum?	1	2	3	4	5	NA
Are grouping techniques used according to developmental levels of the learner (whole group, small group, individuals, partners, teams, cross-age groups)?	1	2	3	4	5	NA
Is the enhancement of individual self-esteem fostered?	1	2	3	4	5	NA
Is the importance of play recognized?	1	2	3	4	5	NA
Are adaptations made to encompass diverse learners?	1	2	3	4	5	NA
Is there evidence of staff collaboration in lessons and planning?	1	2	3	4	5	NA
Do support personnel, regular, and/or special educators team teach?	1	2	3	4	5	NA
Are students' strengths rather than weaknesses emphasized?	1	2	3	4	5	NA
Are the contributions of all students valued?	1	2	3	4	5	NA
Is authentic assessment data gathered for all children (portfolios, progress samples, work samples)?	1	2	3	4	5	NA
Are parents used as resources?	1	2	3	4	5	NA

Teachers' Publishing Group

T: TEAMS

Classroom teachers must be committed to meeting the needs of *all* children in the educational setting. When faced with the challenge of including a child with unique needs and gifts, regular education teachers may doubt their abilities and wonder, "How do I do this? How can I reach 25 other children and yet teach this child with such diverse learning needs? Do I have enough time in my day?" This is the time to introduce teachers to the collaborative team approach, a critical part of the inclusion process. As part of a team, individual members begin to see their roles intertwined as part of the larger scheme of integration.

The team should include the building principal, homebase teacher, special education teacher, instructional consultants, guidance counselors, psychologists, support personnel (speech, Chapter 1, occupational therapist, physical therapist), additional regular educators, parents, and children. Some schools are comfortable including special needs students and peers at team meetings. Children who attend meetings are able to help adults focus on child-centered problems without the use of educational jargon. Many schools begin to include children who are at least nine years old in meetings.

Team members should be notified of date, time, place, agenda and names of those attending an upcoming meeting at least one week in advance. They should receive descriptions and be aware of specific problems and possible outcomes the teacher needs with each case to be discussed. It is helpful to have posted at the meeting site a framework for problem-solving steps and meeting timelines (see page 140). Core members of the collaborative team share responsibilities such as timekeeper, facilitator, note keeper, and case manager.

"The collaborative process encourages staff and parents to share expertise and educational strategies."

The collaborative process encourages staff and parents to share expertise and educational strategies. Team members come together to problem solve, fact find solutions, brainstorm strategies, and target specific implementation dates and responsibilities. The team supports its members while attempting to arrive at a consensus about educational programs and find answers to questions and problems team members face. They begin to share the mottos "All for one and one for all" and "None of us is a smart as all of us."

Collaborative teams allow a group of people to attack problems too large or too overwhelming for individuals to handle alone. The trust developed by a team makes teachers more willing to seek needed support. They begin to see collaboration with staff as an extension of their in-class cooperative learning philosophy. Teams give educators the opportunity to share expertise, build trust, help other staff members, and receive the necessary support in planning programs and designing interventions that will help children succeed.

Tips

1. Meet in a comfortable environment where all participating can see each other.

2. Have name cards visible to help parents associate names and job titles with faces.

3. Send written invitations to parents with date, time, and agenda. Include an RSVP form.

4. Try to keep team size limited to seven members.

5. Allow for all participants to share.

6. Encourage members to arrive on time and stay until the meeting has concluded.

7. Do not attempt to stop and update tardy members.

8. Encourage secretaries to welcome parents and help make them comfortable until the meeting begins.

9. Notify absent members of the meeting outcomes.

10. Share written results of the meetings with all participating members.

11. Encourage teachers to rotate the roles needed at the team meeting.

12. Define goals and objectives for the student before the meeting begins.

13. Develop brainstorming techniques that allow for independent thinking and no put downs.

14. Restate the final consensus for all while emphasizing who is responsible for implementation and by what date.

15. Schedule a follow-up meeting with all present.

16. Enter team meetings on equal footing – no one is an expert.

17. Encourage members to share resources and materials.

18. Check to make sure all team members understand the decisions.

19. Allow for multiple solutions through brainstorming.

20. Value input from all members.

Team Meeting Outline

Team reaches consensus on concerns – two minutes.

Team negotiates student objectives – three minutes.

Gather brief additional input from members – two minutes. (Written information is to be distributed prior to meeting).

Team brainstorms solutions – eight minutes.

Teacher selects appropriate interventions – three minutes.

Refine interventions – three minutes.

Develop action plan/list members' responsibilities to plan – four minutes.

Scheduling Time for Team Meetings

Schools need to develop a creative approach to the team process and the time it involves. Many teachers are willing to serve on teams and bring problems to the team but feel they have no time left in a busy day for teaming. Possible solutions include:

1. Schools can employ a rotating substitute one afternoon a week. This sub would cover classes for teachers, thus freeing classroom teachers to attend meetings. As each meeting concludes, the sub then rotates to another classroom to free that teacher for a meeting.

2. Adjust the daily instructional schedule by shortening lunch and recess and dismissing students earlier each day to allow teachers time for team meetings and collaboration.

3. A parent volunteer group can provide students with assemblies and activities every other Friday afternoon from 2 to 3 p.m. so teachers can attend team meetings.

4. Intermediate classroom teachers can pair themselves up with primary teachers for project days. On the first and third Friday of every month the primary teacher could bring his/her class to the intermediate class from 2 p.m. until dismissal so s/he could meet with the special education staff or attend building-based team meetings. On the second and fourth Friday of the month the intermediate grade students would come into the primary classroom to book share, assist at centers, or help with elaborate art projects. At that time the intermediate teacher could attend meetings.

5. A school may want to schedule one day each month to talk about a specific included child. For example, the first Monday of every month from 8 to 8:30 a.m. the team will meet to discuss how Tommy is doing in the classroom. From 8:30 to 9 a.m. the team will discuss Calvin's progress. By planning ahead monthly for regularly scheduled meetings, teams take time to discuss not only strategies but children's individual successes.

Instructional Support Team Meeting

To the parents of_____

There will be an Instructional Support Team meeting to discuss your

child's progress on_____ at_____ in the

 primary school office.

_____   _____
Classroom Teacher   Date

Please check in with the secretary in the primary office upon your arrival.

- -

☐ I will attend

☐ I will not attend

Signed_____Date _____

Developing Meeting Agenda and Goals

Team Agenda

1. The team will meet on _____ at _____ in _____.
   (date) (time) (place)

2. The child to be discussed is _____ in Room _____.

3. Those in attendance will include (List names and job, such as Mary Smith, physical therapist.)

_____

_____

_____

_____

4. The parents _____will/_____will not attend.

5. The agenda for this meeting is

_____

_____

_____

6. The teacher concerns are:

_____

_____.

7. If you are out of the building and are unable to attend, your input will be taken by proxy. Please send a written report to
_____ before
(case manager)

_____.
(date)

8. Lengthy reports or data should be distributed to all members two days prior to meeting.

Purpose:

The following form may help support teams streamline the process of developing the meeting agenda and goals.

Procedure:

Develop a form to be routed to principal, homebase teacher, special education support personnel, consultants, counselors, and psychologists.

Instuctional Support Team Action Plan

Child's name _____

Classroom Teacher _____

Meeting Date _____

Support Staff _____

Special Education Teacher _____

Goal Area/Objectives	Strategies to Facilitate Implementation	Resources Needed	Person Responsible	Target Date for Implementation to Begin	Comments on Implementation

Teachers' Publishing Group

Support Planning

Student _____

Meeting Goals

See page 191 for an example of how this form can be used.

U: UTILIZING RESOURCES

Educators today often share a common concern – how to utilize resources to assist in inclusion while not draining a district's budget.

A local district that's promoting inclusion must first provide the staff with strong administrative support and leadership. Administrators who are strong believers in inclusion and who are creative problem solvers tend also to be advocates of the teaming process. Such leaders provide the district with a clear mission and a common vision with high educational standards. Not only will they be team players, they will also provide instructional support to teachers, allow for flexible planning time, encourage collaboration, and provide adequate staff development.

Often the most valuable source of expertise is found within the school setting. Many times teachers are reluctant to boast about their skills and knowledge. If there is a teacher in the school who has been trained in teaming, that skill is invaluable when developing building-based teams. Teachers who are knowledgeable in whole language or process writing will be able to assist others with independent reading activities for included children. Teachers who have outside interests and hobbies can be tapped as resources for cooperative learning activities or thematic units. Special educators can provide inservice workshops on special education labels, categories, and special teaching techniques.

"Often the most valuable source of expertise is found within the school setting."

Tips on Utilizing Resources

1. Poll individual teachers to assess individual talent and resources.

2. Encourage community members who have been on the inclusion task force to share the philosophy community wide. Invite them to participate in classroom activities.

3. Develop a section for differently-abled material in the school library devoted to articles, papers, journals, and educational resources for staff, students, and parents.

4. Include peers as resources in IEP and team planning meetings, Circle of Friends (see page 43), MAPS (see pages 81-84), and transition teams as students move from elementary to middle school. Children often recognize a peer's true needs before an adult does.

5. Contact your state department of education for names of inclusion consultants.

6. Organizations such as TASH, CEC, The Inclusion Press (see Organizations and Resources, pages 197-198), or the U.S. Department of Education can provide resources that help teachers develop successful inclusion programs.

Staff Inventory

Some of the best resources available to educational staffs are right within your own school. Inservicing does not always mean looking outside the school for assistance. We applaud the gifts and talents of students while not recognizing our own teaching abilities. A survey like this encourages collegial sharing.

Sharing Your Expertise

Please check the areas that you have received training in and would be comfortable assisting a colleague to develop.

❐ Whole language

❐ Ages and stages of children

❐ Multiage classrooms

❐ Developmental assessments

❐ Hands-on science

❐ Team teaching

❐ Team building

❐ Effective discipline plans

❐ Inclusion

❐ Curricular adaptations

❐ Learning styles

❐ Process writing

❐ Early interventions

❐ Hands-on math

❐ Collaboration

❐ Learning stations

❐ Computers in classes

❐ Life-skills issues

❐ Authentic assessments

❐ Defining gray area children

❐ Multicultural awareness

❐ Assistive communication devices

Please return this to the office. We will be using you as a staff resource person in the near future.

Name_____Class_____

V: VISITATIONS

One of the most reassuring tasks when becoming an inclusive school is visiting a variety of schools where successful inclusion is in place.

When scheduling a visit, request a time when it is permissible not only to observe regular classrooms, but also to share concerns with regular and special educators, Chapter 1 teachers, and support staff. Tape-record or videotape, if permitted, the exchanges with these teachers. Visitors should then be encouraged to share their findings and interviews with their home school, perhaps in a faculty meeting. Invite staff members you've visited to speak to your school. Keep in mind that although your initial apprehensions about inclusion are shared by many, excitement about children's success is contagious and will help ease those anxieties.

"Invite staff members you've visited to speak to your school."

Teachers who visit a variety of inclusive schools find it helpful to use a standard visitation form. By using a questionnaire, staff members are sure to have covered the same topics of concern at all on-site visitations and have an easier time deciding which programs to use as models or which teachers to use as consultants. Those who set up folders for each school visited and include the completed questionnaire, photos, videotapes, and specific interview questions can have at their fingertips a directory of resources ready to use on an individual as needed basis.

On-site Visitation Questionnaire

Name_____ Date of visit_____

Site_____ Location_____

Population_____ Length of project_____

Training staff received_____

_____

_____

1. Describe the program you observed and comment on: the number of identified students involved, the pattern of staff involved, and the number of years the program has been in operation.

2. Is this program based on an integration model or an inclusion model? Are students based in a special education class and mainstreamed for art, gym, and music, or are they totally included in a regular classroom for instruction?

3. Describe the type of instructional and social opportunities available for students with disabilities to be involved with their typical age-appropriate peers.

4. What type of support did you see provided to students with disabilities when they were in social and instructional settings with their peers?

5. Based upon your observation, were students with disabilities successfully supported alongside their peers?

6. What types of instructional opportunities were provided for students with disabilities that were unique to them?

7. As the program continues and evolves, what recommendations can you make for further development or expansion?

8. Describe the interaction you had with regular, special, and support staff, and their personal evaluation of this inclusive project.

9. List three positive outcomes from your interactions and observations.

10. How will you share your findings with your staff?

11. Is this school one that you would encourage others to visit or invite for inservicing your staff? Why or why not?

W: WHY INCLUSION?

Inclusion is the right thing to do. Children belong in neighborhood schools and social settings with peers their own age. We have kept regular education and special education apart long enough. It is time for the two forces to join together, to provide learning and positive social interaction opportunities for *all* children.

A successful inclusive program will help children develop a sense of belonging, acceptance, and community spirit. In such a setting, limitations and labels will no longer drive educational programs. As labels diminish for children, they will also disappear for teachers. Education will become teachers teaching all children rather than "special educators teaching special children."

When the philosophy of acceptance is embraced, teachers' collegial relationships will be strengthened and feelings of isolation diminished.

Inclusion builds the foundation for lifelong friendships. Children will be comfortable with accepting one another regardless of abilities. And, as adults, diversities will be accepted as a natural part of life.

By providing today's children with this opportunity to build a foundation of togetherness and acceptance, tomorrow's adults will have a better chance of developing a more peaceful and harmonious world.

"A successful inclusive program will help children develop a sense of belonging, acceptance, and community spirit."

Inclusive Rationale

- Recognizes that all children learn at different rates.
- Provides age-appropriate classroom settings to challenge all children and frustrate none.
- Fosters self-esteem through individual learning success.
- Encourages cooperative learning for students and collaboration for staff.
- Highlights strengths of learners without focusing on weaknesses.
- Provides accommodations as necessary to enhance learning.
- Embraces diversity and teaches to uniqueness.
- Supports teachers and learners to meet needs of all.
- Encourages social interactions during and after school with nonhandicapped peers.
- Provides opportunity for family participation in schools and neighborhoods.
- Siblings of labeled children begin to see that other children also have siblings with special needs.
- Supports become a service rather than a location.

Working Definition of Inclusion

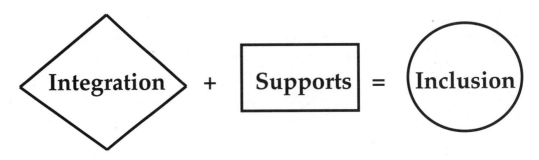

A Letter From Jonathan

The staff has been adequately prepared, the parents have been educated, time has been provided for collaboration and planning, but who remembered to ask the student how it felt to return to the classroom?

Dear World,

I have just spent my first month in my neighborhood school. It was so cool! When I first heard Mom and Dad talking about this, I wanted to jump for joy, but you know that is impossible when you're stuck in a wheelchair. But I sure showed them I was happy by the look on my face.

Before this year, I was sent to a special school with other kids like me. It was an okay place, but we were so much alike that nothing seemed too exciting.

Then Mom and Dad got very interested in my IEP. They made friends with the parents of other kids with IEPs. I think they figured out there are more things I can do rather than the IEP's list of things I can't do. They talked to the principal and the teachers, and then it happened!

It was scary for me at first, but what fun! Now I ride to school with other kids from the neighborhood. My big brother and little sister go with me. But now they don't need to always be explaining me to their friends 'cause now their friends know me!

My classroom teacher is a really neat guy. He lets me sit with all the other kids. The aisles are real wide so I don't bump into everyone! Mr. Norman lets us kids work together in special projects.

My group's always awesome 'cause we help each other and take time to listen. Some days the other kids argue because they all love it when I'm in their group. Raoul says I keep everyone working!

I have other friends coming into Mr. Norman's room to see me. Mrs. Bubb comes to do speech, Mrs. Henninger does muscle exercises, Miss Todd helps me and any other kid who needs help. It seems like they all realize I can learn, but sometimes I learn differently.

I finally have friends who can push my wheelchair. Kids like to sit by me at lunch and in programs. I am even starting to play baseball. Of course I just throw the ball when I'm up to bat, but who cares? I'm one of the guys!

This month has been the best month of my life. People are learning to see me for what I am — a kid who just happens to be in a wheelchair. I know the friends I have now will be my friends for a long time. Who knows, maybe one of them will be my doctor or my secretary when we get old.

Thanks to my mom, dad, and new school, I finally feel like I belong.

Your friend,
Jonathan Ford

X: EXPECTATIONS

Clearly define expectations for all students in the regular classroom setting and develop a set of developmentally appropriate expectations. From this list of projected teaching outcomes, children's appropriate learning goals will spring forth.

Teachers should keep the meaningfulness of learning in mind and ask themselves, "Why am I asking children to learn this? How will it affect their long-term learning?" Children need to understand the reason a particular lesson is being taught.

Regular education teachers should be able to successfully plan thematic units and lessons while feeling comfortable with individual expectations and educational goals. However, faced with the challenge of integrating special needs children into the classroom, some teachers may feel overwhelmed by the fear they can't meet the needs of this diverse population. Each special needs child who is placed in the regular education setting needs to be "set up for success."

The classroom teacher can sit down face-to-face with a special education teacher or support person and share a student's strengths and weaknesses, but the list of weaknesses should be no longer than the list of strengths. The teacher can draw from the special educator's knowledge of the student's performance level and can get help in making curricular adaptations as needed.

The school setting prepares children for community living. All children must leave the classroom ready to be contributing members of society.

"All children must leave the classroom ready to be contributing members of society."

Common Developmental Expectations

Realizing common multiage expectations may help teachers better understand differently-abled children in the regular classroom.

Social Expectations

5-7 year-old:

- Enjoys group as well as solitary play
- Moves away from parallel play
- Realizes that others have feelings and needs
- Expresses feelings openly
- Notices that there is a larger world than his/her own play world
- Understands the need for food, clothing, shelter
- Compares likenesses and differences in others with self
- Empathizes with peers
- Understands simple rules and consequences
- May love you one minute and hate you the next
- Experiences anxiety separation
- Is fickle with friendships
- Feels many things aren't fair
- Attempts to share or take turns
- Attempts to become independent

7-9 year-old:

- Works well in cooperative groups
- Begins to separate work from play
- Realizes what triggers others' feelings, emotions, and needs
- Hesitates to express feelings which may cause embarrassment
- Develops close friends which s/he may monopolize
- Empathizes with peers at a deeper level
- Shows an interest in other cultures and their needs
- Understands rules and consequences, not always eager to abide by them
- Critical of self and others
- Anxious in large groups of unknown people
- Needs to have well developed self-esteem
- Judges self according to adult interactions

Physical Expectations

5-7 year-old:
- Growth rate begins to slow
- Slower improvement in fine motor development and skills
- Awkward use of pencils, scissors, markers
- Developing improved eye-hand coordination
- Difficulty copying from far to near
- Handedness becoming established
- Difficulty with direction words – top left, bottom right, lower corner
- Not comfortable with skipping
- Developing ease with running, climbing, galloping
- More aware of body parts and their usage
- Displays spurts of energy
- Difficult to sit still – movement preferred
- Plays active games with children of the same sex

7-9 year-old:
- Uneven growth spurts
- Appears like arms and legs will outgrow torso
- Eyesight is not firmly developed
- Marked improvement with eye-hand coordination
- Handedness as well as foot preference established
- Awkward posture due to growth spurts
- Able to copy from far to near with ease
- Able to comprehend basic functions of the body in a scientific manner
- Enjoys organized sports and board games
- Able to conserve body energy for appropriate times
- Becomes a risk taker/show-off
- Loyal to friends and teammates

Intellectual Expectations

5-7 year-old:
- Requires hands-on learning
- Understands cause and effect relationships
- Uses oral and beginning written language for expressing learning

- Connects written word to spoken word
- Enjoys drawing to express emotions
- Understands how a book works
- Personalizes vocabulary
- Enjoys being read to
- Can "picture read" a book
- Learning to read
- Substitutes one word for another when reading aloud
- Confuses time elements – yesterday, tomorrow
- Able to state phone number, address, birthdate
- Developing independent thinking – states what s/he doesn't like to eat or wear
- Able to conserve numbers
- Matches numbers to sets

7-9 year-old:
- Enjoys manipulatives for complex thinking problems
- Uses abstract as well as concrete thinking
- More defined oral and written language
- Enjoys words with double meanings
- Writes elaborate stories
- Enjoys a variety of literature
- Able to silently read and comprehend
- Develops reading skills and strategies for decoding
- Increases sight vocabulary
- Able to self-correct when reading aloud
- Reads with expression
- Reads to learn
- Understands time, uses a clock
- Understands money value
- Organizes self and world
- Wants an active role in group decision making

Y: YOUR STRENGTHS

During this intensive systematic change in our schools, it is imperative that teachers do not doubt their own strengths and visions for educating children.

When recent college graduates were asked "Why did you choose teaching?", invariably their responses were: "I love children.""I want to make the world a better place." "I want to assist in producing good and productive citizens.""I enjoy the collegial aspect of helping kids learn.""I love the challenge of designing educational programs to meet the needs of all learners.""I like being a part of a team of educators who are making the world safer." "Kids are great!"These sentiments reflect why people have chosen to teach. Teachers' strengths lie in the fact that they usually do love kids and want to make their world better. They do not go into teaching to help only some children. The educational system that we were plugged into has fostered the feeling that some educators may be more special and more capable of handling children with special needs.

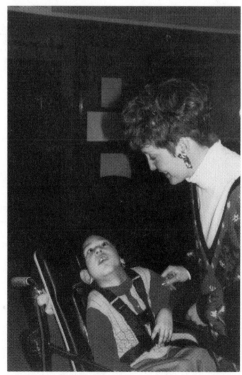

The time is ripe for teachers to validate their own strengths and expertise and to work with others who share their belief in equal rights in education. Our combined knowledge and underlying desire to help children will help make the philosophy of "Collegial support to help all children learn" the reality in our classrooms.

Z: ZERO REJECTION

An inclusive school embraces a philosophy of "zero rejection," which means that no one is shunned from becoming an active participant in his or her home school because of a label. Schools are not inclusive if they say, for example, "We welcome all children back to their neighborhood schools except children who are autistic."

The "principle of partial participation" allows students with severe disabilities to participate in regular classroom activities for part of the day. This enables students to acquire many skills that would allow them to function, in part, in a variety of classroom and after-school programs.

However, it also recognizes that not every child should participate in a regular classroom for 100% of the school day. Schools must take the initial step in bringing children back to their home schools and then begin designing programs which help children succeed in the regular education setting.

By encouraging educators to accept everyone into their schools, while realizing the option of partial participation, staff is encouraging students to increase their personal dignity, their sense of belonging, and their positive self-esteem while giving them the opportunity to earn the respect of peers.

Schools that provide children with systematic and coordinated participation efforts at a young age will increase the likelihood that these individuals will become more than partial participants in many environments as they continue in school and in preparation for adult life.

Tips

1. Allow a child to bypass learning addition or multiplication facts and use a calculator during math class.

2. Allow talking books or taped lessons to assist a child in completing a specific curricular activity.

3. Provide a stamp pad and a name stamp to be used by children who are unable to write their names on papers or library books.

Levels of Student Participation

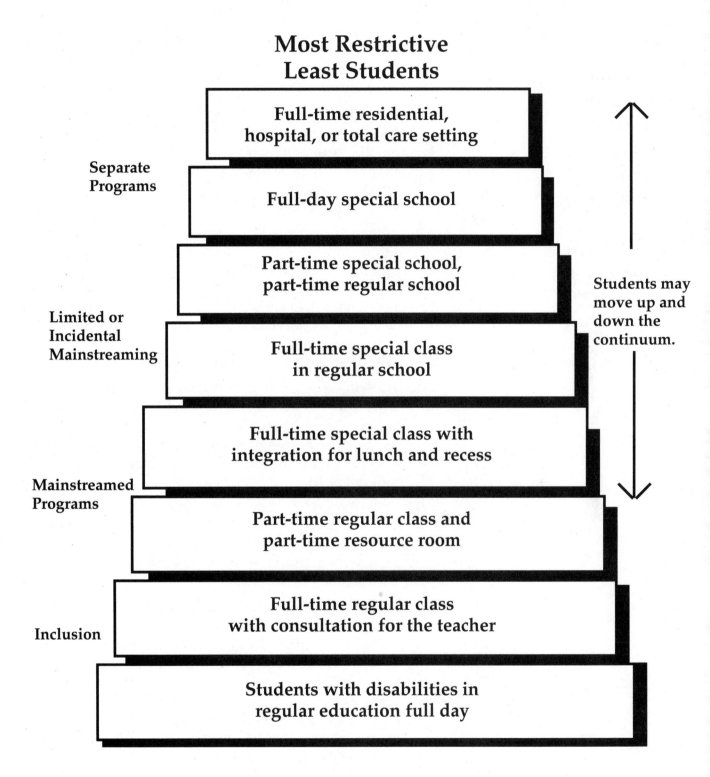

**Most Restrictive
Least Students**

	Full-time residential, hospital, or total care setting
Separate Programs	Full-day special school
	Part-time special school, part-time regular school
Limited or Incidental Mainstreaming	Full-time special class in regular school
	Full-time special class with integration for lunch and recess
Mainstreamed Programs	Part-time regular class and part-time resource room
Inclusion	Full-time regular class with consultation for the teacher
	Students with disabilities in regular education full day

Students may move up and down the continuum.

**Least Restrictive
Most Students**

Determining a Child's Level of Participation

"Is the student able to successfully and actively participate in the regularly designed lesson?"

1. Is the student able to successfully and actively participate in the regularly designed lesson? If so, that student may successfully be included for 90%-100% of the day with the collaborative effort of special and regular education teachers.

2. Does the student need to have adaptations made to the lesson, materials, or classroom expectations? If so, that student will need to have the collaborative efforts of a special and regular teacher, with the special education teacher and/or aide visiting the classroom periodically.

3. Is the student able to participate by working on his/her personal communication, socialization, or motor skills somewhere in the regular classroom while another lesson is taking place? If so, that child may need more than simple collaboration and periodic visits for support. Daily in-class visits from the support staff and regularly scheduled team meetings will need to take place to meet the IEP goals.

4. Does the student need to be working on an entirely different activity while remaining within this group of peers? If so, that child will need the same support as above with possible pull-out time allotted for individual attention as governed by the IEP and student need.

5. Does the student need to be working in a different location in the classroom while meeting individual goals? Inclusion for this child might be social inclusion, with academic goals met in the classroom by the special education staff.

6. Is the student more likely to be successful while completing an educational goal in an out-of-class setting for a specified length of time? Inclusion for this child may mean being with typical classmates for attendance, opening, lunch, recess, art, gym, library, and music. Academic IEP goals may be met in another setting with the child returning to the regular classroom for project-based work, e.g., learning centers, social living, science, and playtime.

Appendix

Take a look at all the previously discussed forms by walking through the inclusion process with Susan Doe, her parents, and her support personnel. Some of these forms are used universally; others are used at the discretion of the school-based team.

Blackline masters of the following forms can be found on the pages listed below:

IEP Inventory — pages 62-64

MAPS Meeting Plan – page 84

Elementary Inventory of Parent Preferences/A Preamble to the IEP — pages 106-112

Student Profile Sheet — page 132

Support Planning — page 145

SAMPLE EVALUATION REPORT

_____INITIAL REFERRAL   _____ RE-EVALUATION

STUDENT NAME: <u>Susan Doe</u>
BIRTH DATE: <u>1/4/84</u>   GRADE: <u>K</u>   SCHOOL: <u>PRIMARY</u>
CURRENT PROGRAM: <u>Regular kindergarten with supplemental</u>
<u>intervention</u>

REASON FOR REFERRAL
Susan was referred for a re-evaluation to develop recommendations concerning placement and intervention as she moves from a developmentally-oriented, half-day kindergarten into an academically-oriented, full-day first grade at the Primary School.

BACKGROUND INFORMATION
Susan is a six-year-old child who was diagnosed soon after birth as having Down Syndrome. Susan and her parents participated in early-intervention programs, and she attended a preschool program for developmentally delayed and normally developing children. Susan has had several major surgeries to repair congenital physical abnormalities, including, most recently, a cerebral vertebrae fusion for which she has needed various devices to support her neck during kindergarten. Her gross and fine motor development has been somewhat delayed as a result of the major surgeries during her early childhood. The results of a psychological evaluation indicate that Susan is functioning within the high subaverage range of ability.

INTERPRETATION OF ASSESSMENT RESULTS:
Parent Interview: In an informal interview, Susan's parents report that their long-range goal for Susan is that she will be able to live and work in their community and that her quality of life will be enhanced by having friends and acquaintances in her home community. They noted that they are sure of Susan's potential in many areas, but they would like her to be both challenged and supported in the academic areas. Her communication skills are of great importance to them because adequate communication skills are necessary both in school and in relationships out of school. The parents are very consistent in providing follow-through at home, and Susan's mother has served as a member of the building-based integration team for the last year. Mr. and Mrs. Doe are very excited about her new ability to use the computer and would like Susan's skills in that area to be utilized.

Previous Educational Performance: This school year, Susan Doe has been enrolled in the afternoon kindergarten with an aide available for support during all activities, including those which took place during several extended school days each week. She participated in all instructional activities with the class, except when receiving therapy on an individual or small-group basis.

She has made satisfactory progress in her IEP goals (which were in the life-skills areas) and in the kindergarten curriculum with adaptations/modifications made as needed.

Teacher Interview/Observation: The kindergarten teacher, Mrs. Black, reports that Susan's ability to learn and recognize sight words puts her near the top of the class in prereading/reading skills. She appears to rely wholly on her visual memory to learn words by sight, rather than using decoding strategies. Mrs. Black considers Susan to be in the lower portion of her class in reading comprehension. Susan enjoys reading and likes "playing teacher," especially reading Big Books to other students.

Mrs. Black also reports that Susan has made satisfactory progress on following rules, increasing her attention span in large-group lessons, and generally following the kindergarten daily routine as part of the whole group. She has concerns about Susan's stamina for the full-day first grade and about her ability to handle the demands of the integrated reading/language arts curriculum.

Ecological/Life-Skills Assessment: An ecological inventory and discrepancy analysis of Susan Doe's current performance indicated the following priority environments and activities for instruction for Susan:

Priority Environments: School and Home

Activities:
- Dressing/undressing (coat, hat, gloves, boots) during arrival, recess and departure, and bathroom times. *
- Playground/indoor recess – improve socialization skills and interactions with other children. *

  *Communication in all activities.

Additionally, the special education consultant and teaching assistant observed the first-grade classroom on several occasions and analyzed each activity in a typical day for the following factors: 1. content area, 2. type of instructional group, 3. length of activity, 4. mode of evaluation, 5. materials used for learning, 6. practice, or evaluation. The special education consultant then compared/contrasted Susan's current repertoire of skills as evidenced in the kindergarten classroom with the demands that would be expected in the typical first-grade classroom.

The results of this analysis indicated that Susan would probably need:
- adaptations to decrease the number and length of "pencil and paper" tasks;
- individualized practice on basic number and math concepts and possibly slower pacing through the math curriculum;
- support/schedule adaptations to maintain her attention through the lengthy, intense morning portion of the schedule.

Attempts were made to work toward some of these goals in the last few months of kindergarten, and Susan has been able to increase the amount of time she participates appropriately in the whole-group situation.

The therapists who are currently serving Susan were asked to assess her abilities and needs in priority activities identified through the ecological analysis.

The speech and language therapist, Mrs. Tutley, reports that Susan has progressed from 1- or 2- word answers to consistently using short (3-5 words) but complete sentences and that Susan is able to expand on ideas in some situations. Her clarity of speech has improved; however, it is still difficult at times to comprehend the message. Susan has also begun to respond to two-step directions in individual or small-group sessions, but often gets confused when more complex directions are given or if she is in a large-group situation.

Susan has been without a neck brace for about 3 months, after having worn one for almost 9 months. The physical therapist reports that she is still strengthening her neck muscles and learning to use her neck for developing some self-confidence on the swings and other playground equipment.

The occupational therapist, Mr. Tomlinson, indicated that although Susan can write legible letters and numbers, she does not have the fluency or stamina to perform the amount of pencil-and-paper tasks required in the first grade. He recommends a combination of working on improving Susan's fluency and stamina and providing alternative modes of performing typical paper-and-pencil tasks.

STRENGTHS
Sight word recognition, excellent visual memory skills, keyboarding and computer use, following routines, learns well through highly structured, systematic instruction.

NEEDS
Fine motor and gross motor skills needed for handwriting and school activities, interactive communication skills, higher-level reading comprehension, motivation to learn math concepts.

RECOMMENDATIONS (TO IEP TEAM)
Based upon the assessment results, the current placement is appropriate to meet Susan Doe's needs and should be continued. The team feels that special education services and supports are still required because Susan's areas of need require a level of support that would not be available in a regular first grade. She needs instruction in critical life-skills areas which are not part of the first-grade curriculum, and she has significant needs in the areas of communication and motor skills. She also needs a variety of adaptations to materials and pacing.

PROGRAM RECOMMENDATIONS
Continue supportive interventions in the typical, appropriate classroom, providing academic learning support for identified reading, math, and handwriting needs. Continue providing life-skills support in areas of communication, dressing, interactive recreation/leisure skills. Analyze first-grade curriculum and determine specific areas in need of adaptations, modifications, or alternative goals based upon Susan's strengths and utilizing technology (computer, word processor, assistive devices).

IEP INVENTORY

Family members fill out the inventory prior to and share it in the IEP meeting.

PARENT QUESTIONNAIRE

Student Name _Susan Doe_ Age _6_

Parent Name _Mr. & Mrs. John Doe_

Address _5 Shadow Lane_

1. List three activities your child takes part in with your family.

   a. _Vacations – Long Island, Cape May_

   b. _Church, Preschool Sunday School_

   c. _Restaurant, Mall, Disney Movies_

2. How extensively is your child involved in these activities?

   Susan is fully included in family activities with John & Me

3. Is your child able to entertain him/herself alone?

   Not well. She prefers to be with me or friends

4. What recreational activities can be implemented at school to improve your child's quality of life?

   Board games, card games, balls, jump rope

5. List your child's three favorite stories

   a. _Jack n Beanstalk_

   b. _Grinch Stole Christmas_

   c. _Ugly Duckling_

6. What reading skills do you see as part of your child's educational plan (listening to stories, identifying story characters, recognizing simple words, sounding out words, reading words in context, recognizing words around the community)?

listening to books on tape, reading alone

7. List three math skills your child demonstrates at home (one-to-one correspondence counting, value of money, making change, telling time, measuring, using a calculator, identifying numerals, writing numerals, adding and subtracting).

Counts to 111, 1 to 1 with numbers to 12, computer, recognizes some out of order

8. Using the examples from number seven, what math skills would you like to see your child acquire this year?

money value, different coins, adding, subtracting facts

9. Describe your child's fine motor skills (button, snap, zip, stringing beads, using writing instruments, tie shoes, coloring, cutting, and pasting). How can the school improve these skills?

Susan has weak fine motor skills. Give her lots of practice that is fun for her.

10. Describe your child's communication skills (speaks in sentences, phrases, or single words, uses sign language, noncommunicative, easily understood).

Susan only speaks in 2 or 3 word sentences. She isn't always understood.

11. Is your child more comfortable communicating with certain family members or peers than others? Please describe.

She is most comfortable talking to me. Friends don't always understand her.

12. Does your child maintain eye contact during communication?

Not at all times

13. Is your child able to follow oral directions? A two-step direction?

Susan is able to follow a 2-step direction with many repetitions or picture clues.

14. List three ways you'd like to see your child's language skills improved.

1. Talk more   2. Be understood   3. Express needs

15. List three social activities you'd like your child to take part in.

1. Brownies   2. Dance lessons   3. Friends to come over

16. Are there any other skills or activities not noted that you would like your child to learn?

Dressing self   Regular Gym Class

17. List three ways you would like to be contacted regarding school information (phone, postcards, weekly diary).

1. Phone at work
2. Daily diary (for first month at least)
3. Post cards would be fun

Note: Many multiage schools use similar questions when discussing placements with parents. Children in a multiage setting may have individualized educational plans in place, regardless of exceptionality.

MAPS Meeting Plan

STUDENT NAME: _Susan Doe_

DATE OF MEETING: _Fall 1993_

THOSE IN ATTENDANCE: _Mr & Mrs. Doe, Ms. Smith,_
Miss Wittle, Mrs. Tutley, Mr. Tomlinson,
Ms. Brown, Ms. Jones

FACILITATOR: _Mrs. Lingle_

RECORDER: _Mrs. Smith_

1. Tell us about _Susan_'s history. Susan experienced a normal birth. We knew she was a Downs Syndrome baby at 5 days. She's been delayed in all developmental areas.

2. What are your hopes and dreams for _Susan_'s future? We want Susan to be self-sufficient in adulthood. We'd like her to have friends and be social. We want her to have a Job.

3. Describe your fears or nightmares regarding _Susan_. Our biggest fear is that she would be alone and unhappy if we were to die.

4. Tell me, who is _Susan_? She is a loving, kind child with some developmental delays

5. In your opinion, what do you think _Susan_ likes. Other than chocolate ice cream, she likes puppies, computers and active children.

6. Speaking positively, what do you see as _Susan_'s strengths, gifts, talents? Her smile, her hugs and her empathy towards others, also her visual memory.

7. What physical, social, emotional, or academic needs does _Susan_ have? Occupational therapy for fine motor skills. Physical therapy for gross motor skills. Susan needs speech and language and preparation for life skills.

8. Working as an educational team, how can we provide an ideal day for

Susan here at school? Allow her to be in a regular class for most of the day. Improve her independence. Encourage use of Th computer and foster friendships.

9. As a parent describe your child in five words.

Happy, loving, helpful, stubborn (at times), active

Elementary Inventory of Parent Preferences

Student Name: _Susan Doe_

Parent's Name: _John & Jane Doe_   Student Age: _6_   Grade: _Going to 1st_

Preschool Attended: _Easter Seals Preschool_   Phone: (home) _____ (work) _____

     Previous School Attended: _____

Your response to the following questions will help identify areas that should be included on your child's Individual Education Plan for this year. This information will be used as a *starting point* in the development of your child's Individual Education Plan.

Community Living Skills

Activity/Skill	Does student currently do this?	What kind of help is needed?	Would you like student to work on this?
Walk in neighborhood	(Y) N		Y N
Obey traffic signs	Y (N)	not independent	(Y) N
Eat at fast food restaurant	(Y) N		Y N
Eat at sit down restaurant	(Y) N	much patience	Y N
Eat in cafeteria	(Y) N		Y N
Use vending machines	Y (N)		(Y) N
Can locate house	(Y) N	only from down street	Y N
Say address	Y (N)		(Y) N
Say phone number	Y (N)		(Y) N
Recognize community helpers	(Y) N	visual clues	Y N
Can locate school	Y (N)	reinforcement	(Y) N
Can locate classroom	(Y) N	doesn't know name	(Y) N
Can locate school bus/bus number	(Y) N	only if the bus is in the same spot	Y N
Other _____	Y N		Y N

Living Skills

Activity/Skill	Does student currently do this?	What kind of help is needed?	Would you like student to work on this?
Food Preparation			
Use correct utensils	Ⓨ N	can't use knife	Ⓨ N
Prepare simple snacks	Ⓨ N	I get out supplies	Ⓨ N
Pack lunch with assistance	Y Ⓝ	All supplies out —	Ⓨ N
Eat unassisted	Ⓨ N	Still can't make sandwich	Y N
Clothing Care			
Separate clothes	Y Ⓝ		Ⓨ N
Fold clothes	Y N	with 2 choices	Y Ⓝ
Choose daily outfits	Y Ⓝ	Doesn't know when to wear what	Ⓨ N
Identify types of clothes	Ⓨ N		Ⓨ N
Cleaning			
Could hand wash dishes	Y Ⓝ		Y Ⓝ
Make bed	Y Ⓝ	Someone must stand next to her	Y Ⓝ
Sweep floor	Y Ⓝ		Ⓨ N
Set/clear table at mealtime	Y Ⓝ		Ⓨ N
Take out garbage	Y Ⓝ		Y N
Dust furniture	Y Ⓝ		Y Ⓝ
Straighten bedroom	Y Ⓝ		Y Ⓝ
Pick up toys	Ⓨ N		Y Ⓝ

Living Skills

Activity/Skill	Does student currently do this?	What kind of help is needed?	Would you like student to work on this?
Other Domestic Skills			
Care for house plants	Y (N)		(Y) N
Care for pet	Y (N)		(Y) N
Help rake leaves	Y (N)		(Y) N
Pick flowers/vegetables	Y (N)		(Y) N
Other: _____	Y (N)		(Y) N

Leisure Skills

Activity/Skill	Does student currently do this?	What kind of help is needed?	Would you like student to work on this?
Gross Motor Skills			
Skip	Y (N)	Lacks coordination	(Y) N
Talk a walk	Y N		Y N
Hop	Y (N)		(Y) N
Play with frisbee	Y (N)		(Y) N
Swim	Y (N)		(Y) N
Play team sports	Y (N)	needs a large, soft ball	(Y) N
Throw a ball	(Y) N		(Y) N
Catch a ball	(Y) N		(Y) N
Games/Crafts/Hobbies			
Read or look at books	(Y) N	Looks only	(Y) N
Play computer games	Y (N)		(Y) N
Play video games	(Y) N		Y (N)
Play card games	(Y) N	Only easy ones Slap Jack	Y N

Leisure Skills (Continued)

Activity/Skill	Does student currently do this?	What kind of help is needed?	Would you like student to work on this?
Games/Crafts/Hobbies (Continued)			
Play board games	Y (N)	Can't take turns	(Y) N
Can play alone	Y (N)		(Y) N
Can share with others	Y (N)		(Y) N
Listen to stories	(Y) N		(Y) N
Choose favorite story	(Y) N	Cat in Hat	(Y) N
Has favorite song/music	(Y) N	Big Bird Sing Along	(Y) N
Use paste	Y N		(Y) N
Use scissors	Y N		(Y) N
Do puzzles	Y N		(Y) N
Can build with blocks	(Y) N	Only 3-cube tower	(Y) N
Musical Activities			
Respond to music	(Y) N		(Y) N
Use cassette	(Y) N		(Y) N
Use radio	(Y) N		(Y) N
Listen to music	(Y) N	Loves jazz	Y N
Attend Events/Places			
Go to mall/shopping	(Y) N	Susan goes almost everywhere with us. She shouldn't need these here.	Y (N)
Go to library	(Y) N		Y (N)
Watch sporting event	(Y) N		Y (N)
Go to a movie	(Y) N		Y (N)

Leisure Skills (Continued)

Activity/Skill	Does student currently do this?		What kind of help is needed?	Would you like student to work on this?	
	Y	N		Y	N
Other:					
	Y	N		Y	N

Personal Skills

Communications Skills

	Y	N		Y	N
Answer telephone	Ⓨ	N	only with picture clues	Y	Ⓝ
Dial telephone	Y	Ⓝ		Ⓨ	N
Talk with friends/family on phone	Ⓨ	N		Y	N
Relay personal information (name, phone number)	Y	Ⓝ		Ⓨ	N
Seek information when needed	Y	Ⓝ	Cries instead of asking for help.	Y	N
Seek help when needed	Y	Ⓝ		Ⓨ	N

Self Care Skills

	Y	N		Y	N
Dress self	Y	Ⓝ		Ⓨ	N
Button self	Y	Ⓝ		Ⓨ	N
Zip self	Y	Ⓝ		Ⓨ	N
Tie shoes	Y	Ⓝ	Limit choices	Ⓨ	N
Select appropriate clothes	Ⓨ	N		Ⓨ	N
Locate restrooms	Ⓨ	N		Ⓨ	N
Wash hands and face	Ⓨ	N		Ⓨ	N

Personal Skills (Continued)

Activity/Skill	Does student currently do this?	What kind of help is needed?	Would you like student to work on this?
Brush teeth	(Y) N		(Y) N
Bathe/shower alone	Y (N)	hand-over-hand	Y N
Other: We'd like Susan to be Self-Sufficient	Y N		Y N

Work Skills

Work Habits

Activity/Skill	Does student currently do this?	What kind of help is needed?	Would you like student to work on this?
Complete given chores	(Y) N	Small direction	Y N
Follow verbal directions	Y (N)	only 1 step	Y N
Follow written directions	Y (N)	No skills	Y N
Clean up toys/room	Y (N)	Once in a while	Y N
Ask for assistance when needed	Y (N)	Lacks verbal skills.	Y N
Other:	Y (N)		Y N

Looking into the Future

1. What accomplishments would you like your son or daughter to have after elementary school?

   ☒ Acceptance of self, others

   ☒ Appreciation for self-accomplishments

   ☒ Awareness of others' abilities and gifts

   ☒ Achievement on an individual academic basis

   All of these are vital to Susan, John, and me.

2. Describe how you will encourage the development of friendships with your son/daughter (in school and after school):

   I will be room mother. I would like Susan to join Brownies and Tumble Bunny Dancers.

3. How would you like to be involved in the educational process at our elementary school?

   Parent volunteers
   Team meetings
   Receive weekly updates   Book Sharing Mom

Student Profile Sheet

Student Name __Susan Doe__ Homebase Teacher __Miss Wittle__
Special Education Teacher __Ms. Smith__
Education Paraprofessional __Mrs. Jones__
Will the aide accompany the student?   Yes   ⓃⓄ

Strengths	Weaknesses
Strong visual memory Enjoys school	Delayed fine, gross motor skills Tires easily Socialization

Goals for	Suggested Activities for
Physical Education: Allow Susan to participate with age-appropriate peers.	**Physical Education:** Provide quiet activities along with high activity levels.
Music: Have Susan participate in singing rhythms, and whole group instruction	**Music:** Peer tutors, modeling, quiet singing after rhythms
Art: Develop cutting ability	**Art:** Provide adapted scissors as needed. Hand-over-hand instruction
Library: **Computer:** } Be an active participant in a typical classroom.	**Library:** **Computer:** } Limit paper pencil work with her interests

Strategies for behaviorial intervention

Use of positive reinforcement

Student interest

Pets
Books

Medical concerns/Procedures to implement

N/A

SAMPLE IEP - LIFE SKILLS AND LEARNING SUPPORT

NAME: Susan Doe   **SCHOOL DISTRICT ADDRESS:** 5 Shady Lane
SCHOOL: Primary Elementary, Anywhere, OH
PHONE: 555-123-4567   **IEP MEETING DATE:** 8/7/90
AGE: 6.9 years   **DATE OF BIRTH:** 1/04/84

DATE WHEN SERVICES AND PROGRAMS WILL BEGIN: 9/09/90

TYPE OF SERVICE: Learning Support and Life-Skills Support

LEVEL OF INTERVENTION: Supplemental Intervention in the Regular Class (itinerant)

LOCATION OF INTERVENTION: Regular Neighborhood School

ANTICIPATED DURATION OF SERVICES AND PROGRAMS: Ongoing

RELATED SERVICES
Speech Therapy: 30 min/per week, individual session in regular classroom.
Language Therapy: 30 min/per week, individual session. 30 min/per week, group session.
30 min/per week, group session in regular classroom with nondisabled peers during
language arts "workshop" time.
Occupational Therapy: 45 min/per week, individual session.
Physical Therapy: 45 min/per week, individual session.

*All therapists will consult and collaborate with other team members to ensure that there is
consistency in Susan's program.

INTEGRATION IN REGULAR CLASSROOM
Susan is in regular first grade on a full-time basis with an instructional assistant in the
classroom for support as needed/planned. She will be "pulled out" for individual therapy
sessions on an as-needed basis with the majority of services provided in the first grade.

ADAPTATIONS/MODIFICATIONS TO REGULAR EDUCATION CLASS:
A full-time instructional assistant is assigned to the first-grade class in which Susan is
enrolled. This assistant's primary responsibility is to provide support to Susan Doe as
needed. The assistant works with other students in the class as the teacher feels appropriate. Other modifications are described in the context of the goal to which they relate.

Susan has limited fine motor endurance due to physical limitations and recent surgery. An
Apple computer and/or a portable word processor will be made available as an alternative
to pencil/paper tasks. Additionally, seating adaptations will be made to facilitate proper
posture for handwriting.

EXIT CRITERIA: When Susan can progress adequately in regular education without the
support of an instructional assistant and special education consultant.

PARENT PARTICIPATION: As part of the multidisciplinary team, Susan's parents completed an initial survey regarding their priorities for Susan's educational program for this year. They also participated in a planning meeting at which the team came to a consensus on priority goals for Susan.

INSTRUCTIONAL AREA: Handwriting Skills

PRESENT LEVEL: Susan can currently color and print letters of the alphabet. (She prefers to use upper-case letters but is able to copy.)

ANNUAL GOAL: To improve handwriting skills.

SHORT-TERM OBJECTIVES: Susan will form the upper- and lower-case letters and numbers as needed for each writing task throughout the school day, forming letters and numbers which are appropriate size for the task and which are legible as evaluated weekly based upon teacher observation and a criterion checklist, meeting 100% of the criteria for four consecutive weeks. Legibility will also be evaluated based upon informal opportunities for the teacher, instructional assistant, parent and peers to read and comprehend Susan's appropriate written products with 100% of written products legible. Susan will take part in journal writing on a daily basis. Samples of Susan's work will be maintained in her portfolio.

SPECIALLY DESIGNED INSTRUCTION: Susan needs a seating adaptation to allow her feet to rest on a stable surface so that she maintains a posture which will maximize her endurance for the fine motor skills involving handwriting, (phone book, box, stools). Susan will handwrite brief answers required as part of instructional activities (several words or numbers, filling in blanks) as well as specific handwriting practice exercises. When the composition of sentences and paragraphs is required, Susan will use a word processor to complete the activity. As her endurance for handwriting increases, she may begin to use the word processor less often. During journal time, Susan will be able to use a processor or picture writing as needed.

INSTRUCTIONAL AREA: Reading Skills

PRESENT LEVEL: Susan has a strong sight word vocabulary and good visual memory skills. She currently participates in most of the classroom reading and whole language activities with some fine motor adaptations and modifications.

ANNUAL GOAL: To improve reading skills.

SHORT-TERM OBJECTIVES: Susan will develop reading skills following the course of the first-grade curriculum. Susan will be exposed to the written word in literature, language experience activities, journals, books on tape. She will focus on sight word vocabulary, phonetic skills, writing, and expanding on ideas, with 100% accurate performance on a subset of the first-grade reading goals based upon teacher observations, evaluations, oral responding, and writing samples in her portfolio.

SPECIALLY DESIGNED INSTRUCTION: Alternative instructional and evaluation strategies which utilize Susan's strengths (e.g., good visual memory and strong sight word vocabulary) will be developed to teach portions of the curriculum which are more difficult for Susan to master (e.g., phonetic skills, sequencing, comprehension). Dictation exercises and other activities which require fine motor skills will be modified and/or reduced, and Susan will use a word processor to complete writing exercises.

INSTRUCTIONAL AREA: Math Skills

PRESENT LEVEL: Susan can currently count numbers to 100, group sets, and do some simple addition facts using visual aids.

ANNUAL GOAL: To improve math skills

SHORT-TERM OBJECTIVES: Susan will complete addition and subtraction facts to 10 with 100% accuracy based upon teacher evaluation of work, tests, and oral responding on a weekly basis.

Susan will tell time to the hour and with 100% accuracy based upon teacher observation.

Susan will identify coins (penny, nickel, dime, quarter) with 100% accuracy based upon teacher evaluation of work performed.

SPECIALLY DESIGNED INSTRUCTION: Susan will participate in large-group math instruction with adaptations support as needed for each lesson; however, when the students are doing individual practice or review, Susan will receive individualized instruction and practice with the instructional assistant. The pace at which Susan is instructed will be adjusted to allow her sufficient practice to master math skills.

INSTRUCTIONAL AREA: Domestic Skills/Dressing

PRESENT LEVEL: Susan can presently put on and take off a coat or other forms of outer wear that she can put over her head using a flip motion. She can also perform most undressing skills required for using the toilet. She can unzip, zip, and unbutton large loose buttons. Susan ended the kindergarten year with 83% accuracy on her undressing/dressing instructional program. The areas that require more support are: fastening buttons, hook type closures, and pulling down and pulling up tighter fitting pants and tights after using the toilet.

ANNUAL GOAL: To improve dressing skills.

SHORT-TERM OBJECTIVES: Susan will perform dressing/undressing skills that are required during the normal course of the school day with 100% independent performance. This includes: putting on and taking off her coat and any outer wear she wears to school; opening and closing fasteners; pulling down and pulling up tightly fitting clothes in order to use the toilet.

SPECIFICALLY DESIGNED INSTRUCTION: The occupational therapist will work with Susan on developing an age-appropriate method for putting her coat on independently. The occupational therapist will work with the team, including parents, so that Susan practices this technique whenever she has to put her coat on. Susan will be given a few extra minutes to begin to prepare for going home and to use the bathroom while she is learning these skills.

INSTRUCTIONAL AREA: Communication Skills

PRESENT LEVEL: Susan generally speaks in short but complete sentences and can expand on ideas and topics in some situations. Although her clarity of speech has improved, her message is sometimes misinterpreted or not understood.

ANNUAL GOAL: To improve communication skills.

SHORT-TERM OBJECTIVES: Susan will extend her current vocabulary and the average length of her sentences in a manner that can be understood by her peers and teachers. Susan will increase the average length of sentences and will incorporate new words into her vocabulary, using each word in a given language group and in classroom conversation on 5 occasions.

Susan will use verbal language to initiate/sustain social interactions through conversations in speech and language instructional sessions and in classroom activities. Evaluation will be based upon a checklist which categorizes types of communication (statement of needs, requests, and social interaction initiations/responses) and quality of communication (was message understood by intended listener?). She will increase the daily and weekly frequency of each type of communication by 50% and will communicate understandable messages to intended listeners 90% of the time.

Susan will follow complex, multi-step directions and respond appropriately to peer or teacher initiated questions or comments, in speech and language instructional sessions and in classroom activities, following directions and responding to questions or comments 90% independently in both planned and unplanned situations.

SPECIFICALLY DESIGNED INSTRUCTION: Classroom teacher and speech and language therapist will identify specific times and activities in the daily schedule when strategies for mediating Susan's communication will be implemented in the context of the ongoing activity.

A language checklist will be completed bimonthly during language group with nondisabled peers and during other classroom activities which require verbal communication to assess the generalization of communication skills across settings.

The teacher, assistant, and speech/language therapist will teach peers to ask Susan to repeat things that they do not understand, and they will be "coached" on ways to involve Susan in conversations so that she has maximal opportunities to practice communication skills.

INSTRUCTIONAL AREA: Recreation/Leisure Skills

PRESENT LEVEL: Susan currently plays on the playground by participating in the same or similar activities as the other students but without any sustained interactions. She enjoys running and will climb on some of the playground equipment, but she has worn a neck brace which limited her physical abilities for a large part of last year and was not able to fully participate in most playground activities. She is also able to participate in familiar table games.

ANNUAL GOAL: To improve recreation/leisure skills.

SHORT-TERM OBJECTIVES: Susan will independently participate in playground games and activities such as: using the swings and slide, playing jump rope and hopscotch with nondisabled peers, and be evaluated by physical education teacher and playground aides twice per week.

Susan will independently participate in unfamiliar table games/cards games with nondisabled peers across settings (e.g., home, indoor recess, free time) with 100% independent turn taking and rule following for 3 new games weekly to measure frequency of turn taking and percentage of rule following.

SPECIALLY DESIGNED INSTRUCTION: For each activity, the physical therapist will evaluate Susan's physical limitations and will plan the level of participation which is appropriate and the level of assistance needed (i.e., due to difficulties in maintaining balance, Susan needs to be "spotted" when climbing the ladder to the slide). The physical therapist will consult with the classroom teacher regarding limitations/adaptations.

The recess aides will provide planned support during recess, and the physical education teacher will also provide instruction during gym class on some skills that Susan will need on the playground.

The speech and language therapist will work with the recess aides to develop strategies for encouraging Susan to play interactively with other students and to encourage the other students to involve Susan in their play activities.

IEP TEAM ALSO CONSIDERED:

✓ Adaptive Phys. Ed. **Not needed**
___Extended School Year
___Vocational Education
___Behavior Programs
___Enrichment/Advancement

___Assistive Devices
___Graduation Planning
___Preparation for Adult Life
___Student Health Concerns
___Other (Specify) **OT PT**

MEETING PARTICIPANTS

Life-skills teacher: _Brenda Smith_

Parent: _John Doe_

Parent: _Jane Doe_

Principal, LEA Representative: _Mrs. Lingle_

First-grade teacher: _Miss Wittle_

Speech clinician: _Mrs. Tutley_

O.T. Mike Tomlinson

P.T. Peggy Brown

T. Assistant Loretta Jones

Support Planning

Student Susan Doe

Meeting Goals	Writing Skills (seating adaptations, word processor, pictures)	Reading (Tapes, Processing time)	Math (manipulatives, computer)	Domestic Life/Skills (one-to-one)	Communication (picture tapes)	Thematic Units (Playground activities)	Gross Motor
Home base Teacher	✓	✓	✓		✓		
Sp. Ed. Teacher		✓	✓	✓	✓		
Teacher Asst.	✓		✓	✓	✓		
Peer Tutor	✓		✓		✓		
Parent Volunteers		✓	✓		✓	✓	
Cooperative Lrn. Groups	✓	✓		✓	✓	✓	
Speech/Lang Therapist					✓		
Occupational Therapist	✓			✓			
Physical Therapist						✓	
Adaptations							

Instructional Schedule for Susan Doe

Teacher: Ms. Smith/Assistant Mrs. Jones   Grade: 1st   Room 1

	Monday	Tuesday	Wednesday	Thursday	Friday
8:30 - 9:00	----------------Opening, Rug Time, Songs, Finger Plays, Calendar, Weather Chart--------------------				
9:00- 9:15	------------------Bathroom, Drinks * Teaching Assistant Mrs. Jones as needed------------------------				
9:15 - 10:30	Whole Language * Ms. Smith (in-class support)	Block: Journals Peer Tutors Grades 4, 5	Language Experience *Ms. Smith	Charts, Process Writing, Word Processor Peer Tutors Grades 4, 5	*Ms. Smith
10:30 - 11:00	Book Sharing Parent Volunteer	Silent Reading, mini-lessons, phonics, vocabulary review, speech/language Mrs. Ford	Mrs. Einsel	Mr. Papas	* Mrs. Tutley
11:00 - 12:00	Lunch/Recess Monitor as needed	(OT, PT will consult with recess aides) Peer Support	Recess Aides	Teaching Assistant	
12:00 - 1:00	Manipulative Math Cooperative Groups Ms. Smith (in-class support)	Computer Math * Mrs. Jones		Life Skill Application (shopping, store in room)	
1:15 - 1:30	--Bathroom, Drinks * Mrs. Jones --				
1:30 - 2:15	Art	Music	Phys. Ed.	Library	Phys. Ed.
2:15 - 3:00	Thematic Units OT Mr. Tomlinson	Social Living Cooperative Groups	Science Large Group Projects	Health	Communication PT Ms. Brown
3:00 - 3:30	Speech * Mrs. Tutley	Centers: Games	Speech *Mrs. Tutley	Centers for Social Interaction	Speech *Mrs. Tutley
	--------Dismissal with age-appropriate, typical peers, assisted with dressing as needed--------				

Professional Bibliography

Albert, Linda. *Teacher's Guide to Cooperative Discipline – How To Manage Your Classroom and Promote Self-Esteem.* Circle Pines, MN: American Guidance Service, 1989.

British Columbia Ministry of Education. *Supporting Learning: Understanding and Assessing the Progress of Children in the Primary Program.* Victoria, British Columbia, 1991.

Curran, Lorna. *Cooperative Learning Lessons for Little Ones: Literature-based Language Arts and Social Skills.* San Juan, Capistrano: Resources for Teachers, 1991.

Fagan, S.A.; Graves, D.L.; & Tressier-Switlick, D. *Promoting Successful Mainstreaming: Reasonable Classroom Accommodations for Learning Disabled Students.* Rockville, MD: Montgomery County Public Schools, 1984.

Grant, Jim, and Johnson, Bob. *A Common Sense Guide to Multiage Primary Programs.* Columbus, OH: Teachers' Publishing Group (in press).

Harwell, Joan. *Complete Learning Disabilities Handbook.* New York: Simon & Schuster, 1989.

Jenkins, J., and Jenkins, L. "Peer Tutoring in Elementary and Secondary Programs." In *Effective Strategies for Exceptional Children*, edited by Meyer, E.L.; Vergason, G.A.; and Whelan, R.J., 335-354. Denver, CO: Love Publishing Co., 1988.

Lipsky, D.K., and Gartner, A. *Beyond Separate Education – Quality Education for All*. Baltimore: Paul H. Brookes, 1989.

McGregor, G., and Vogelsberg, R.T. *Transition Needs Assessment for Parents*. Philadelphia, PA: Temple University, 1989.

Pennsylvania Department of Education. *Gateways – An Integration Initiative for Students with Severe Disabilities*.

Rainforth, Beverly; York, Jennifer; and McDonald, Cathy. *Collaborative Teams for Students with Severe Disabilities*. Baltimore: Paul H. Brookes, 1992.

Roach, Virginia. "Special Education: New Questions in an Era of Reform." *Issues in Brief* Vol. 11, No. 6 (1991).

Rosner, Jerome. *Helping Children Overcome Learning Difficulties*. New York: Walker, 1979.

———. *Visual Motor Program, Auditory Motor Program*. New York: Walker, 1979.

Routman, Regie. *Invitations, Changing as Teachers and Learners*. Portsmouth, NH: Heinemann, 1991.

Society For Developmental Education. *Creating Inclusive Classrooms: Education for All Children*. Peterborough, NH, 1994.

Stainback, S., & Stainback, W. *Support Networks for Inclusive Schooling*. Baltimore: Paul H. Brookes, 1990.

———. *Curriculum Considerations in Inclusive Classrooms: Facilitating Learning for All Students*. Baltimore: Paul H. Brookes, 1992.

Stainback, S.; Stainback, W.; and Forest, M., eds. *Educating All Students in the Mainstream of Regular Education*. Baltimore: Paul H. Brookes, 1987.

Thousand, J.S., and Villa, R.A. "Strategies for Educating Learners with Severe Disabilities Within Their Local Home Schools and Communities." *Focus on Exceptional Children*, Vol. 23, No. 3 (1990): 1-24.

Vail, Priscilla. *Gifted, Precocious, or Just Plain Smart, A Story for Puzzled Parents*. Rosemont, NJ: Programs for Education, 1987.

Vandercook, T., and York, J. "A Team Approach to Program Development and Support." In *Support Networks for Inclusive Schooling: Interdependent Integrated Education*, edited by Stainback, W. and Stainback, S., 95-122. Baltimore: Paul H. Brookes, 1990.

Villa, R.; Thousand, J.; Stainback, W.; and Stainback, S. *Restructuring for Caring and Effective Education: Administrative Strategies for Creating Heterogeneous Schools*. Baltimore: Paul H. Brookes, 1992.

Wilcox, B., and Bellamy, G.T. *The Activities Catalog*. Baltimore: Paul H. Brookes, 1987.

York, J.; Vandercook, T.; MacDonald, K.; and Wolff, S. "Instruction in Regular Education Classes for Students with Severe Disabilities: Assessment, Objectives, and Instructional Programs." In *Strategies for Full Inclusion*, edited by York, J.; Vandercook, T.; MacDonald, C.; and Wolff, S., 83-89. Minneapolis: Institute on Community Integration, 1990

Children's Bibliography

Bagert, Brod. *Chicken Socks and Other Contagious Poems*. Honesdale, PA: Boyds Mills Press, 1994.

Brimmer, Larry Dane. *Max and Felix*. Honesdale, PA: Boyds Mills Press, 1993.

Browne, Anthony. *Piggybook*. New York: Alfred A. Knopf, 1986.

Cheripko, Jan. *Voices of the River*. Honesdale, PA: Boyds Mills Press, 1994.

Cohen, Miriam. *First Grade Takes a Test*. New York: Greenwillow, 1980.

———. *It's George*. New York: Greenwillow, 1980.

———. *No Good In Art*. New York: Greenwillow, 1980.

———. *When Will I Read?* New York: Greenwillow, 1977.

———. *Will I Have a Friend?* New York: Macmillan, 1967.

Dodds, Bill. *My Sister Annie*. Honesdale, PA: Boyds Mills Press, 1993.

DeFossard, Esta. *Dinah, the Dog With a Difference*. Milwaukee: Garth Stevens, 1988.

dePaola, Tomie. *The Art Lesson*. New York: Putnam, 1989.

Howell, Troy. *Ugly Duckling*. New York: Putnam, 1990.

Fossler, Joan. *Howie Helps Himself*. Chicago: Whitman, 1975.

Kroll, Virginia L. *Naomi Knows It's Springtime*. Honesdale, PA: Boyds Mills Press, 1993.

Lasker, Joe. *He's My Brother*. Chicago: Albert Whitman Co., 1974.

———. *Nick Joins In*. Chicago: Albert Whitman Co., 1980.

Mariotti, Mario. *Humands*. San Diego: Green Tiger Press, 1983.

———. *Humages*. San Diego: Green Tiger Press, 1985.

Martin, Bill Jr. *Knots on a Counting Rope*. New York: Holt, 1987.

Mayer, Mercer. *Little Monster's Bedtime Book*. New York: Golden Press, 1978.

Muldoon, Kathleen. *Princess Pooh*. Chicago: Albert Whitman, 1989.

Peet, Bill. *The Ant and The Elephant*. New York: Houghton Mifflin, 1972.

Sobol, Harriet Langsom. *My Brother Steven Is Retarded*. New York: Macmillan, 1977.

Spier, Peter. *People*. New York: Doubleday, 1980.

Stein, Sara Bonnett. *About Handicaps*. New York: Walker, 1974.

Organizations/ Resources

Paul H. Brookes Publishing Co.
Box 10624
Baltimore, MD 21285-0624

Center for Success in Learning
1700 Preston Rd., #400
Dallas, TX 75248

Centre for Integrated Education and Community
24 Thome Crescent
Toronto, Ontario M6H 2S5

CH.A.D.D. – Children with Attention Deficit Disorders
499 NW 70th Ave., Suite 308
Plantation, FL 33317

Council for Exceptional Children
1920 Association Drive
Reston, VA 22091

Gateways Technical Assistance Initiative
5347 William Flynn Highway
Gibsonia PA 15044-9644

Inclusion Press
24 Thome Crescent
Toronto, Ontario M6H 2S5

Institute on Community Integration
University of Minnesota
109 Pattee Hall
150 Pillsbury Drive
Minneapolis, MN 55455

Kids on the Block Puppets
3509 M. Street, NW
Washington, DC 20007

Learning Disabilities Association (LDA)
4156 Library Road
Pittsburgh, PA 15234

Literacy Labels
    Book A: Things in the Classroom
    Book B: Things at Home
    Book C: Fun Things
    Book D: Things We Eat and Drink
    Book E: Things We Hear
    Book F: Tools We Use
Available from:
Essential Learning Products
P.O. Box 2590
Columbus, OH 43216-2590

Missouri Parents Act (MPACT)
8631 Delmar, Suite 300
St. Louis, MO 63124

National Center for Learning Disabilities (NCLD)
99 Park Ave.
New York, NY 10016

National Down Syndrome Congress
1605 Chantilly Drive, Suite 250
Atlanta, GA 30324

PEAK (Parent Education and Assistance Program)
6055 Lehman Dr., Suite 101
Colorado Springs, CO 80918

TASH – The Association for Persons with Severe Handicaps
11201 Greenwood Ave. North
Seattle, WA 98133

About the Author

Gretchen Goodman

Gretchen Goodman has been an early childhood educator in Pennsylvania since 1973. She has worked in a variety of schools and classroom settings including preschool, kindergarten, pre-first, first, and second grades. Gretchen has served as coordinator of summer school to provide enrichment as well as "safety net" activities for children of all ages and backgrounds.

Currently she is an instructional support teacher who works closely with parents and teachers to develop successful learning and behavioral strategies for primary school children. Gretchen is a consultant for The Society For Developmental Education. She loves traveling around the country to work with teachers who are faced with the challenge of educating all children in the regular classroom.

Gretchen lives in Lancaster, Pennsylvania with her husband Harry, who is an elementary school principal, their two children, Ryan and Aimee, and her dog Bubba, who does flips in the air when Gretchen returns from a trip.